“Working A

Military” Revisited

Spouse Employment in the 2000 Census Data

Nelson Lim, Daniela Golinelli, Michelle Cho

Prepared for the Office of the Secretary of Defense

Approved for public release; distribution unlimited

RAND NATIONAL DEFENSE RESEARCH INSTITUTE

The research described in this report was prepared for the Office of the Secretary of Defense (OSD). The research was conducted in the RAND National Defense Research Institute, a federally funded research and development center sponsored by the OSD, the Joint Staff, the Unified Combatant Commands, the Department of the Navy, the Marine Corps, the defense agencies, and the defense Intelligence Community under Contract DASW01-01-C-0004.

Library of Congress Cataloging-in-Publication Data is available for this publication.

ISBN: 978-0-8330-4118-0

Published 2007 by the RAND Corporation
1776 Main Street, P.O. Box 2138, Santa Monica, CA 90407-2138
1200 South Hayes Street, Arlington, VA 22202-5050
4570 Fifth Avenue, Suite 600, Pittsburgh, PA 15213-2665
RAND URL: http://www.rand.org/
To order RAND documents or to obtain additional information, contact
Distribution Services: Telephone: (310) 451-7002;
Fax: (310) 451-6915; Email: order@rand.org

Preface

This study updates the analyses of the previous RAND Corporation study *Working Around the Military: Challenges to Military Spouse Employment and Education* (Harrell et al., 2004), and revisits the gaps in employment and earnings between military and civilian spouses as well as the demographic and contextual differences that may be associated with those gaps. Like the earlier study, this one responds to the recognition that military readiness and retention of service members depend to some extent on the quality of life for members' families, and that an important element of quality of life for military spouses is employment. Yet information on spouse employment and earnings has been less than complete. *Working Around the Military* (and some notable predecessors by other researchers) made considerable strides toward achieving a more thorough understanding. That RAND study, however, was based on the 1990 census and was restricted, insofar as inferences from census data were concerned, to military wives. The current document repeats and extends the census-based analyses of military wives using data from the 2000 census and also reports the first census-based results for military husbands. This study should be of interest to military policymakers, advocates for military families, military service members and their spouses, and those in the analytic community who study military families and/or wage and employment gaps, in particular gaps among women.

The research was sponsored by the Office of the Under Secretary of Defense for Personnel and Readiness and was conducted within the Forces and Resources Policy Center of the RAND National

Defense Research Institute, a federally funded research and development center sponsored by the Office of the Secretary of Defense, the Joint Staff, the Unified Combatant Commands, the Department of the Navy, the Marine Corps, the defense agencies, and the defense Intelligence Community. Comments are welcome and may be addressed to Nelson_Lim@rand.org. For more information on RAND's Forces and Resources Policy Center, contact the Director, James Hosek. He can be reached by e-mail at James_Hosek@rand.org; by phone at 310-393-0411, extension 7183; or by mail at the RAND Corporation, 1776 Main Street, Santa Monica, California 90407-2138. More information about RAND is available at www.rand.org.

Contents

Figures

Tables

Summary

Previous studies have shown that military wives—women married to U.S. military service members—are more likely to be unemployed than their civilian counterparts (Grossman, 1981; Hayghe, 1974; Schwartz, Wood, and Griffith, 1991; Payne Warner, and Little, 1992; Wardynski, 2000; Hosek et al., 2002; and Harrell et al., 2004). Those who are employed earn less on average than do civilian wives. These studies, however, insofar as they are based on large, representative samples, rely on information that is now somewhat dated, and they have little to say about military husbands. The purpose of the current study is to remedy these deficiencies by repeating earlier analyses of military wives using data from the 2000 census and by extending those analyses to military husbands. Specifically, we seek to determine the following:

- Background characteristics of military and civilian spouses that are potentially related to employment and earnings (e.g., race/ethnicity, education, mobility, and location).
- Employment and earnings status of military and civilian spouses, in general and for each service.
- Trends in all of these variables since 1990.
- The impact of individual and contextual characteristics[1] of military and civilian spouses on employment disparities.

[1] We use the phrases "individual and contextual characteristics" and "background characteristics" interchangeably throughout this document.

Background Characteristics of Wives

Civilian and military wives differ in ways that could have implications for their employment status. According to the 2000 census data, military wives are more racially and ethnically diverse and are better educated than civilian wives. They also tend to be younger than civilian wives and are more likely to be rearing young children. Thus, military wives appear to be at different stages in their life cycles than civilian wives. Military life-style demands also appear to set military wives apart from civilian wives. Military wives are much more likely to relocate than their civilian counterparts and to be located near metropolitan areas, contradicting the common perception that military bases are located predominantly in rural and remote areas.

For a few of these factors, trends either have been flat since 1990 or have been changing similarly for both civilian and military wives. However, the probability of locating in metropolitan areas for civilian wives is increasing to resemble the rates for military wives; the age gap between military and civilian wives is wider in 2000 than in 1990; and the likelihood of having a young child at home has decreased for civilian wives while remaining the same for military wives. All of these differential trends suggest the potential for a worsening employment situation for military wives relative to that of civilian ones.

Employment Status and Earnings for Wives

According to 2000 census data, military wives are less likely to be employed than civilian wives and more likely to be unemployed. Military wives also earn less than civilian wives. Of the military wives, Navy wives are the most likely to be in the labor force and also most likely to earn the most. However, with the exception of a substantially lower unemployment rate for Air Force wives than for those married to other servicemen, differences among services are generally small. None of the individual service employment statistics are as favorable as that for civilians.

National earnings comparisons might be biased if military wives tend to live in areas with lower (or higher) wages. We thus compared civilian and military wives according to where they fell across the overall wage-earning distribution for each metropolitan area and aggregated the results.[2] Military wives are more likely than civilian wives to fall in the bottom 30 percent of the distribution of all wage earners and less likely to be in the top 40 percent. Differences across services are small, but Army wives appear to have a slightly more favorable earnings distribution than wives of other servicemen; Marine Corps wives, a slightly less favorable one.

We repeated the metropolitan-level analysis for different levels of education, from those with no high school diploma to those with a bachelor's degree. Accounting for educational attainment in the metropolitan-level analysis produces more accurate comparisons of military and civilian wives' wages since wages are often positively associated with education. For wives of equivalent education, military wives were again more likely than civilian wives to fall near the lower end of the wage distribution and less likely to fall toward the higher end.

Labor force participation rates are similar between 1990 and 2000 for both civilian and military wives. Unemployment rates, however, are down substantially for all wives, but particularly for Army wives, who have the highest rates. Hourly wages (unadjusted for inflation) are up for civilian wives and for wives across the military services. The wage distribution analysis using 2000 data reveals a slight improvement in the wage distribution of military wives compared with that of a decade ago.

---

[2] This analysis is intended to demonstrate the relative earnings of military wives compared to civilian wives within the same metropolitan area and is not part of the propensity score (look-alike) analysis.

Background Characteristics and Employment Measures for Husbands

Because our sample size for military husbands is smaller than that for military wives, we could not obtain reliable results at the level of the individual service, so we report differences between civilian husbands and military husbands as a whole. Like military wives, military husbands are less likely to be white and are more educated than civilian husbands. They are also more likely to have a young child at home and to relocate more often than civilian husbands.

Like military wives, military husbands have less favorable employment status and earnings than civilian husbands: Their labor force participation and employment rates are slightly lower and their unemployment rate is much higher. They have a substantially lower hourly wage rate and yearly income. The national wage-rate result is confirmed by the metropolitan-area analysis:[3] Military husbands are more likely than civilian husbands to fall into the bottom 40 percent and less likely to be into the top 30 percent of the wage distribution for all workers.

Impact of Individual and Contextual Characteristics on Employment

Wives

Using the propensity score ("look-alike") analysis,[4] we assessed the impact of individual and contextual characteristics on employment. The look-alike analysis, as the name suggests, isolates the effect of observable background characteristics on employment conditions of military spouses by comparing them with civilian spouses whose back-

[3] Again, this analysis is intended to demonstrate the relative earnings of military husbands compared to civilian husbands within the same metropolitan area and is not part of the propensity score (look-alike) analysis.

[4] Appendix D of Harrell et al. (2004) explains technical aspects of the propensity score analysis. Readers may also refer to McCaffrey et al. (2004) and Barsky et al. (2002).

ground characteristics are similar.[5] The look-alike analysis thus ensures that any remaining differences in employment conditions between "look-alike" civilian spouses and their military spouse counterparts could not be attributable to differences in individual and contextual characteristics that we were able to include in the analysis. The second bar for each military service in Figure S.1 illustrates employment rates for civilian wives who share the same observable characteristics (e.g., age, education, and location) as military wives.

Generally, the look-alike civilian wives have employment outcomes similar to those of civilian wives as a whole. The background factors we considered, therefore, do not explain much of the difference between civilian and military wives; these results suggest that most of the differences in employment rates and hourly wages may be due to unobserved factors, which may include differing tastes for work or possible bias among employers. Regarding hourly wages, for instance, one can see in Figure S.1 that civilian wives earned $12 on average in 2000 whereas military wives earned around $9 on average. The bars for look-alikes, however, demonstrate that civilian wives who look like military wives (i.e., who have similar levels of educational attainment, a similar distribution among races, etc.) are earning close to $12. The actual wage differential, therefore, cannot be explained by the available background variables and may be due to unobserved factors. In other words, even when comparing likes with likes, military wives earn less than their civilian counterparts.

In 1990, the look-alike civilian wives' average hourly wage was slightly higher than the average hourly wage of civilian wives. In the 2000 census, however, wages of civilian wives and look-alike civilian wives were comparable, suggesting that military wives are no longer more advantaged than civilian wives in terms of what their wages would be if they were not married to military servicemen.

5 See Table 1.2 in Chapter One for the list of variables included in the look-alike analysis. Results of the propensity score analysis are in Tables A.1a–A.1d in the appendix.

Figure S.1
Hourly Wages Among Civilian, Military, and Civilian Wives Who Look Like Military Wives, 1990 and 2000

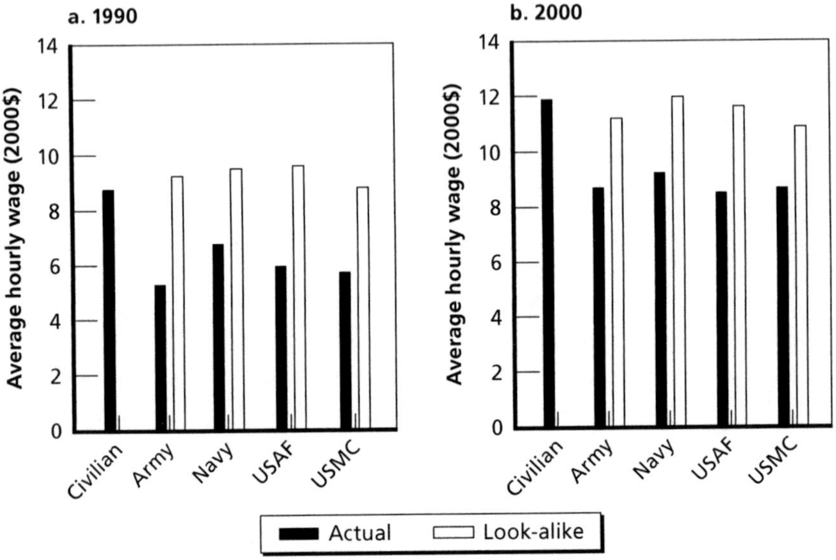

RAND *MG566-S.1*

Regarding unemployment, where higher rates indicate worse conditions, background characteristics explain some of the difference between civilian and military wives (see Figure S.2). In the case of Army wives in 2000, for instance, 4 percent of the civilian look-alike wives in the labor force were unemployed. This is 1.5 percentage points higher than unemployment for the general population of civilian wives. The observed gap between military and civilian wives, however, is about 3 percentage points, which is double the gap between look-alike civilian wives and civilian wives in general. Thus, about half of the observed gap is explained by background characteristics.

Figure S.2
Percentage Unemployed Among Civilian, Military, and Look-Alike Civilian Wives, 1990 and 2000

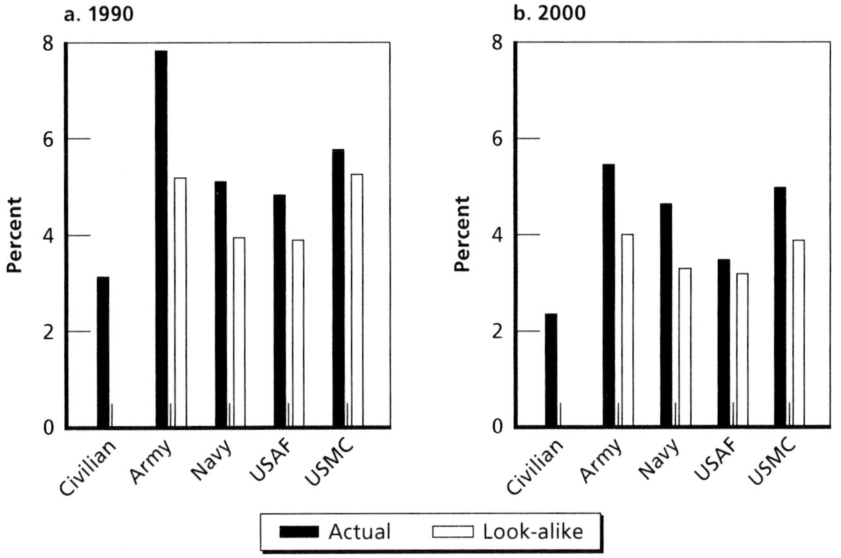

RAND *MG566-S.2*

Husbands

For military husbands, the look-alike analysis revealed that the gap between military and civilian husbands in employment rate is actually smaller than it would be if civilian husbands looked like military ones; the observed gap understates the disparities between civilian husbands and military look-alike husbands. However, background differences explain about half of the difference in yearly income, less than half of the difference in unemployment rate, and most of the difference in the hourly wage rate. In other words, although civilian husbands who look like military husbands are more likely to find jobs than civilian husbands, they tend to be paid less. This trend may be associated with such observable factors as education, race and mobility. Military husbands tend to be more educated than civilian husbands. They are, however, less likely to be white and are more likely to relocate often. Both factors may have an adverse effect on military husbands' wages.

Conclusion

The updated analysis using data from the 2000 census confirms findings previously reported in Harrell et al. (2004). The demographic and employment trends of military and civilian spouses from a decade ago still hold true in general. Military spouses continue to be at a relative disadvantage in the labor market compared with civilian spouses.

The recommendation of Harrell et al. (2004) to address military childcare availability and affordability, as well as that of Hosek et al. (2002) regarding mobility and geographic location of military families, must be recognized as mechanisms designed to reduce the portion of employment disparities that can be explained by observable characteristics. Even if these policies and programs were enacted and were successful at reducing the gap in employment outcomes, they would not affect the portion of the gap that is caused by such unobserved factors as employers' perception of military spouses and the spouses' "taste" for work. For instance, the look-alike analyses on the military wives' unemployment rates (see Figure S.2) suggest that policies and programs aimed at reducing the unemployment rates of military wives may succeed in narrowing the observed gap. However, they would not eliminate the portion of the gap that is attributable to unobserved characteristics, to the extent that they are impractical to modify by policy changes or are resistant to such changes.

An exception would be if observed characteristics are correlated with the unobserved factors. Then any improvements based on an observed characteristic may also affect a correlated unobserved factor, which would further reduce the employment disparities between military and civilian spouses. More data and analysis are needed to better understand what the unobservable factors are, how they may be correlated with other factors, and how they affect employment outcomes. This study also found that certain employment outcomes may be more sensitive to policy interventions that are based on observable characteristics, to the extent that change is desired. One may see larger policy effects on outcomes with military-civilian gaps that are partly or mostly explained by observable characteristics than on outcomes with gaps that cannot be explained with available data. For instance, policies that target such demographic disparities as mobility, location, and childcare may significantly affect the unemployment rate of military spouses, but the same military spouses' hourly wages may still remain unchanged.

Acknowledgments

We are grateful to Aggie Byers and Jane Burke of our sponsoring office for their support and assistance provided during this research. This work benefited from interaction with the Department of Defense Spouse Employment Working Group.

This research benefited from the assistance and intellectual contributions of many RAND colleagues, including Amy Cox, Amelia Haviland, James Hosek, Gregory Ridgeway, Martha Timmer, Yang (Gilian) Lu, James Chiesa, and Christina Pitcher.

Abbreviations

CPS	Current Population Survey
DoD	U.S. Department of Defense
GED	General Equivalency Diploma
IPUMS	Integrated Public Use Microdata Series
MSA	Metropolitan Statistical Area
PUMS	Public Use Microdata Samples
USAF	United States Air Force
USMC	United States Marine Corps

CHAPTER ONE

Introduction

Employment disparities between military and civilian spouses have been well documented in a growing number of studies (Grossman, 1981; Hayghe, 1974; Schwartz, Wood, and Griffith, 1991; Payne, Warner, and Little, 1992; Wardynski, 2000; Hosek et al., 2002; and Harrell et al., 2004). Military spouses[1] are less likely to be employed and more likely to be actively seeking work than civilian wives; even those who are employed earn less than their civilian counterparts. These employment disparities have generated interest among military leadership and policymakers alike (U.S. Department of Defense [DoD], 2004b; Henderson, 2006).

This study provides an updated analysis of military and civilian spouses' employment conditions using the latest population census (2000). It includes a review of employment conditions for military husbands, who were previously excluded due to limited availability of data. The study also embarks on an in-depth examination of the nature of the various factors that contribute to employment disparities. This update on employment disparities can help distinguish between the reality of military spouse employment and the perceptions of unfavorable employment conditions for military spouses. Understanding the differential impact of contributing factors is critical for all stakeholders because not all the employment disparities may be (1) attributable to observable factors or (2) responsive to improvement measures, such as targeted programs or policies. The findings will be particularly helpful

[1] In this study, *military spouses* are civilians who are married to members of the U.S. Armed Forces.

for policymakers who are interested in evaluating the effectiveness of various policy options, as well as for the research community interested in further inquiry.

The analytical approach of this report closely mirrors the approach taken by Harrell et al. (2004), who used data from the 1990 population census. In fact, as the title suggests, this report can be viewed as a sequel to the census analysis in Harrell et al. (2004).[2] In comparing new results with results from Harrell et al. (2004), we observed changes in employment disparities between military and civilian spouses from 1990 to 2000.

Explanations of Employment Disparities Between Military and Civilian Spouses

The existing studies of employment disparities between military and civilian spouses imply various reasons for differences in the groups' employment conditions. We briefly review some of the leading explanations[3] in this section. Some of these reasons are easy to infer and to verify; others are difficult to empirically investigate. Our study attempts to account for the factors that can be explained by the available survey data (i.e., factors related to life-cycle and military demands) and discusses the implications of unobservable factors that also contribute to employment disparities (i.e., factors related to the labor market and individual tastes for work).

Life-Cycle Factors

First of all, in general, civilian and military spouses are at different stages of life-cycle development. Generally, civilian spouses tend to be older than military spouses. Given their age, military spouses are

---

[2] Harrell et al. (2004) also included detailed analysis of more than 1,100 interviews with military spouses about their education and employment experiences.

[3] Researchers have applied similar explanations to disparities in labor market conditions across race, ethnicity, and gender. For example, Neal (2004) discusses various predictors of women's labor force outcomes, differences between different groups of women, or women and men, and related analysis and measurement issues.

more likely to be accumulating skills and work experience, developing their careers, and raising young children at home. Civilian spouses, on the other hand, are more likely to have stable employment and accomplished careers, and less likely to have young children at home. Additionally, military spouses are more likely than civilian spouses to be engaged in educational activities, both as a result of age and also as a result of generational trends—postsecondary education is more common now than it was 10 or 20 years ago. The impact of life-cycle factors can be analyzed by using the data from the census and the DoD Military Spouse Surveys.[4]

Mobility, Location, and Other Demands of the Military Life Style

Military families move frequently and often long distances. Preparing and managing these moves take time and effectively prevent military spouses from engaging in labor market activities. For most military spouses, these moves also mean losing a job and having to find another. Military spouses whose professions require certifications and licenses bear additional burdens of renewing these professional credentials at the new location. In short, these moves can disrupt not only the accumulation of skills and work experience but also career development.

The perceived remote and rural location of many military bases has also been suggested to affect employment outcomes for military spouses (Hosek et al., 2002). Some military spouses find that their skills and experience are not valued in certain labor markets, which may necessitate a career change, temporary employment in an unrelated field, or opting out of the labor force.

The unique aspects of military life also compound employment difficulties for military spouses. The military belongs to a class of social

---

[4] DoD periodically surveys active-duty personnel and their spouses to assess attitudes and perceptions of military life. The information is used to assist in development of policies and programs that aim to improve the military work environment and living conditions of military families. The latest survey results are from 1999. For more information, see U.S. Department of Defense, 2002.

institutions that sociologists call "greedy institutions"[5] (Segal, 1986). Strong demands of the military on service members often spill over onto the families of service members. Given service members' demanding military work schedule, military spouses often must bear a larger share of parenting responsibilities—especially during long deployments of service members. Similarly, military spouses often take greater responsibility for moving. Moreover, unlike civilian couples, who can make relocation decisions considering advantages and disadvantages for all family members, military couples must move according to the timing and placement of the service members' new assignment. The impact of mobility and location can be estimated by using data from the census and the 1999 Military Spouse Survey; the impact of other demands of military affiliation is more difficult to investigate because of lack of data.

Labor Market Factors

Aside from factors associated with life cycles and demands of military affiliation, the labor market also influences employment outcomes of military and civilian spouses. The influences of the labor market factors are in turn shaped by local and federal labor policies, such as minimum wage policy and living wage initiatives. Therefore military spouses' experiences of the effect of the labor market factors may vary across locations and time. Taking the labor policies as exogenous factors, two main explanations of labor market factors have been suggested in the literature: the concept of low-wage equilibrium (Hosek et al., 2002) and a theoretical framework based on subjective matching of workers and jobs.

The low-wage equilibrium framework is derived from an application of the labor economic theory in which wages (i.e., price) are determined by supply and demand for labor (i.e., goods or services). The demand function reflects the relationship between how much labor is

---

[5] These institutions, according to Lewis A. Coser (1974, p. 4), "seek exclusive and undivided loyalty and they attempt to reduce the claims of competing roles and status positions on those they wish to encompass within their boundaries. Their demands on the person are omnivorous."

desired by employers and the wages they are willing to offer; the supply function represents the relationship between the amount of labor that workers are willing to supply based on the available wages. In this framework, employers' wage offers reflect the (marginal) productivity of individual workers. The market-clearing wage is the equilibrium price at which there is no more excess demand or supply.

The low-wage equilibrium describes a situation in which the market-clearing wage is lower than it would be otherwise, perhaps due to mutual disinvestment of employers and workers, as Hosek et al. (2002) hypothesized. Military spouses may be willing to accept lower wages as a trade-off for longer job searches, and employers may offer lower wages in anticipation of military spouses' mobility and other competing demands that are placed upon them.

The second alternative uses a theoretical framework of gender and racial inequality in the labor market (Hodge, 1973; Reskin and Roos, 1990) that implies the existence of labor and job queues that generate and perpetuate inequality. Unlike the low-wage equilibrium explanation, this framework does not assume that the labor market is driven by wages, reflecting the (marginal) productivity of individual workers. Instead, it views the labor market processes as the matching of two sorted queues: labor and jobs. The process of sorting is critical, since the ordering dictates which groups are matched with which jobs. Ordered from most to least desirable, employers tend to hire the workers who are ranked as high as possible in the labor queue, and workers accept the jobs that are ranked as high as possible in the job queue. Given the lack of accurate and complete information about workers' productivity and jobs' quality, the sorting and matching process is essentially subjective. For instance, employers use their prejudices in their sorting of workers from the most to the least desirable. Individuals who are at the bottom of the labor queue are "last hired and first fired." And the wages of these individuals are lower than of those who are higher up in the queue. Using this theory, Thurow (1975) suggested that blacks were more unemployed than whites because employers ranked them below whites in the labor queue, and Reskin and Roos (1990) found that within and across occupations, men are higher in the labor queue than women and thus are ensured the most desirable and rewarding jobs.

Within this framework, we can postulate that employers place military spouses at the tail of the labor queue, based on the information they have to facilitate the sorting process. This placement can explain why military spouses are less likely to be hired and less likely to receive wages comparable to those of their civilian counterparts. The differential placement of these two groups in the queue does not necessarily reflect actual productivity of their members.

Unlike explanations based on demographic factors and residential mobility, the explanation based on the existence of a low-wage equilibrium is not readily verifiable, since information on employers' decision to offer and spouses' decision to accept lower wages does not exist. Analysts must indirectly infer its existence from patterns based on empirical results (Hosek et al., 2002. p. 83). Similarly, it is difficult to confirm the existence of labor and job queues with currently available data. The labor and job queue framework would be more feasible to analyze if data on the information used in the sorting process can be collected.

Taste for Work

Another possible explanation that may explain the different employment outcomes for military and civilian spouses relates to the two groups' "taste" for work, implied by the military spouses' decision to marry service members and the families' decision to stay with the military. For instance, one may argue that, based on military spouses' decision to marry (and remain married) to service members, military spouses are willing "to live in remote areas, to forgo personal opportunity and gain, or to rear a family within the support structure provided by the military" (Hosek et al., 2002, p. 19). Wives who place greater emphasis on labor market participation and believe that job opportunities outside of the military are greater than those within military life may either not marry service members or persuade them to leave the military.

The most difficult challenge in investigating employment disparities between military and civilian spouses is to isolate the magnitude of the disparities that can be attributed to military service. The reason for this difficulty is that service members (and their spouses) are "self-selected" to be part of the U.S. military, which has been an all-voluntary force since 1973. Survey data, including the census, do not contain information about the life-style tastes and preferences needed to verify such an explanation. We can, however, glean clues of the plausibility (or implausibility) of taste-based explanations by comparing employment conditions among military spouses. If the preference for military life is associated with employment outcomes, we should see the nature of this association by comparing labor market behaviors of older and younger military spouses. Older military spouses have been with the military longer and have proven their preference for military life by their decision to remain in it. Younger military spouses, on the other hand, may still be learning about military life and may not yet have formed a preference for it. Harrell et al. (2004) found that older military spouses are more likely to be employed and are less likely to be looking for work than younger military spouses; among those who are employed, they earn higher wages, compared to younger military spouses. These age-related differences persist even after controlling for employment-related characteristics (Harrell et al., 2004). These results suggest that the preference for military life does not lead to a weaker attachment to labor market activities.

Summary

Generally, we can group explanations that have been offered for employment disparities between military and civilian spouses into those that can be verified by available data sources and those that cannot be verified because they require data that have not yet been collected. Using the census data, for example, we can measure the impacts of life-cycle factors and residential mobility on labor market disparities of military and civilian spouses. But employers' attitudes and military spouses' taste for work have not yet been observed and would be problematic to investigate. Isolating the effects of the various factors can effectively inform policies that aim to close the gap in employment outcomes between military and civilian spouses. Understanding the importance of unobservable factors that influence labor market outcomes can lead to key data collection and research activities.

Method and Approach

Data from the 2000 Population Census

This study used data from the 2000 U.S. Census Public Use Microdata Sample (PUMS) from the Integrated Public Use Microdata Series (IPUMS).[6] From available samples, we chose the sample that represents 5 percent of the U.S. population in 2000.[7] To study military spouses, we kept all couples from the 5 percent sample where one spouse was a civilian and the other was either a civilian nonveteran or a member of the military (Army, Navy, Air Force, Marines, or Armed Forces—branch not specified). We excluded couples if either spouse was in the Coast Guard, National Guard, or Reserves or if the spouse of interest was not of working age or was under 18 or over 65. To create comparison groups of civilian wives and husbands, we sampled 20 percent of civilians from the 5 percent PUMS.[8] From those civilians, we selected husbands and wives who were married to nonveteran civilians. (For more information about the PUMS, the reader should consult the U.S. Census Bureau's Web site [www.census.gov] and the IPUMS Web site [www.ipums.org]).

---

[6] Data from the decennial censuses from the Bureau of the Census in the U.S. Department of Commerce have advantages over other data sources such as the Current Population Surveys (CPS) and the Department of Defense's own Military Spouse Surveys. The sample size of military spouses in the census data is considerably larger than that in other data sources, allowing detailed analyses across military services. Moreover, the quality of demographic and migration information available in the census data is comparable to (if not better than) that of alternative data sources.

[7] Harrell et al. (2004) used both the 1 percent sample and the 5 percent sample of the 1990 PUMS. This gave the study additional observations for military spouses. Unfortunately, because of changes in variable definitions associated with the metropolitan areas in the census, we could not combine those two samples from the 2000 PUMS.

[8] The PUMS database contains a variable called, SUBSAMP, which allocates each household to one of 100 subsample replicates, randomly numbered from zero to 99. Each subsample is nationally representative and preserves all stratification of the sample from which it is drawn. Users who need a representative subset of a sample should use SUBSAMP to select their cases. For example, to randomly extract 10 percent of the cases from a sample, select any 10 of the 100 subsamples (http://www.ipums.org/usa/htechnical/subsampa.html).

We selected 20 of the 100 subsamples for civilian spouses and adjusted the sampling weights by multiplying them by five.

Table 1.1 shows the numbers of observations by subgroups. We had nearly 340,173 civilian wives, 449,255 civilian husbands, 19,676 military wives, and 1,466 military husbands. Given the sample size for military wives, we were able to conduct separate analyses for military wives by their husbands' military services, but we had to group all military husbands together to get a sample large enough for statistical analyses.

Table 1.2 shows the variables used in this study. For outcome (or dependent) variables, we examined various employment conditions of military and civilian spouses: employment, unemployment, weeks worked, number of usual hours worked, annual income, and hourly income. In addition, for those spouses living in metropolitan areas, we measured their relative positions in hourly as well as annual income distributions of their local metropolitan labor force. For explanatory variables, we were able to measure a variety of individual-level characteristics of military and civilian couples that are related to employment conditions. These measures include educational level, school enrollment, age, having a young child (or young children) at home, and having moved in the past five years. Finally, we had contextual variables representing the nonmetropolitan status (rural or urban) of individuals' residence and the population size of the metropolitan areas. All these explanatory variables are included in the propensity score (or look-alike) analysis.

Table 1.1
Number of Observations by Military Status and Services

	Wives	Husbands
Civilian	340,173	449,255
Military	19,676	1,466
Army	6,656	488
Navy	5,284	362
Air Force	5,598	555
Marine Corps	2,138	61

Table 1.2
Definitions of Variables Constructed from the 2000 PUMS

Variable	Definition
Outcome Variables	
Spouse employed	Employed if currently employed in civilian job or has a job but not working
Spouse unemployed	Currently does not have a job, is looking for a job, and has not yet found one
Spouse weeks worked	Spouse's weeks worked in 1999
Spouse usual hours worked	Spouse's usual hours worked per week in 1999
Income	Spouse's 1999 annual wage income
Hourly income	[1999 annual wage income] / [weeks worked in 1999 x usual hours worked per week in 1999]
Hourly wage deciles	Spouse's position in the distribution of hourly wage of the local metropolitan area—deciles are computed based on hourly wage for all people age 18–65 who are working
Annual income deciles	Spouse's position in the distribution of annual income of the local metropolitan area—deciles are computed based on hourly wage for all people age 18–65 who are working
Explanatory Variables	
Spouse's education	Mutually exclusive categories: No high school diploma or GED Earned high school diploma or GED; no college education Some college or associate's degree; no bachelor's degree Earned bachelor's degree; no graduate education Graduate or professional school education
Spouse's age	Measured in years
Spouse's race	Mutually exclusive categories: White African-American Hispanic Asian Native American/Eskimo Other
Has young children	True if spouse has at least one child under the age of six

Table 1.2—Continued

Variable	Definition
Moved in past five years	Mutually exclusive categories: Did not move in the past five years Moved in state Moved across states Moved, from abroad
Spouse's school enrollment	Mutually exclusive categories: Not attending school Enrolled in public school Enrolled in private school
Contextual Variables	
Nonmetropolitan status	Household not in a metropolitan area
Metropolitan area size	Survey-weighted number of people in metropolitan area
Metropolitan area size—working age people	Survey-weighted number of people age 18–65 in metropolitan area

Propensity Score (or Look-Alike) Analysis

In this study, the primary goal of our statistical analysis is to isolate the effect of military service on employment conditions of military spouses. As discussed before, military spouses are worse off than their civilian counterparts in all indicators of employment conditions. We cannot, however, readily attribute these employment disparities to military service alone without a rigorous analysis, because military and civilian spouses are different in many characteristics that are strongly associated with employment conditions. A rigorous analysis of these labor market disparities must address whether or not these differences in individual and contextual characteristics of military and civilian spouses account for the observed employment disparities.

Following Harrell et al. (2004), we chose the propensity score analysis to accomplish this task. And like Harrell et al. (2004), we use the less technical term "look-alike analysis" to describe this methodology.[9] The look-alike analysis, as the name suggests, isolates an effect of military service on employment conditions of military spouses by comparing them with their "look-alike" civilian spouses. The look-alike analysis thus ensures that any differences in employment conditions between look-alike civilian spouses and their military spouse counterparts could not be attributable to group differences in observable[10] individual and contextual characteristics. The same observable characteristics are included in the look-alike analysis for both wives and husbands.

We constructed a group of look-alike civilian spouses for the comparison by applying the propensity scores, which reflect how similar a civilian spouse is to a military spouse. These scores range from zero to one. Civilian spouses with higher propensity scores are more similar to military spouses than those civilian spouses with lower propensity scores. We then used the propensity scores as weights to construct a comparison group of civilian spouses for each group of military spouses—four groups of military wives and one group of military husbands.

We demonstrate the power of propensity scores to create look-alike groups whose characteristics are similar to targeted military spouses in Table 1.3, which shows distributions of residential migration experiences of military wives, their look-alikes who are civilian wives, and civilian wives in general. For example, a majority (53.9 percent) of civilian wives responded that they had not moved in the past five years, whereas only one in seven (14.2 percent) military wives responded similarly in 2000. As we discussed above, this difference in residential migration is a potential explanation for employment disparities between these two groups. Using the propensity scores, we constructed a look-alike group of civilian wives. The residential migration experience of look-alike civilian wives is remarkably similar to that of military wives—the dis-

---

9 Appendix D of Harrell et al. (2004) explains technical aspects of the propensity score analysis. Readers may also refer to McCaffrey, Ridgeway, and Morral (2004) and Barsky et al. (2002).

10 By *observable,* we mean observable in available data—in particular, census data. *Unobservable* factors are those for which data are not available. Theoretically, unobservable factors could possibly be observed through instruments not yet fielded.

Table 1.3
Residential Migration Among Military Wives, Their Look-Alike Civilian Wives, and Civilian Wives, 2000 (%)

	All Military Wives	Look-Alike Civilian Wives	Civilian Wives
Residential migration			
No move in the past five years	14.2	14.5	53.9
Intrastate move	19.7	19.7	35.0
Interstate move	55.5	55.2	7.9
Moved abroad	10.6	10.6	3.2

tributions of migration categories are practically identical. Therefore, if we see any differences in employment conditions between these two groups, we can be confident that the differences are not because military wives moved frequently and often long distances. This reasoning applies to all the characteristics we included in the look-alike analysis.

Limitations of the Look-Alike Analysis

We have shown that comparisons of employment conditions between military wives and their look-alike civilian wives effectively controlled for differences between military and civilian wives in the observable characteristics that we included in the look-alike (or propensity score) analysis. We caution the reader that the census variables used in the analysis might not accurately measure the underlying constructs and therefore the look-alike analysis might not achieve balance of such constructs. Therefore, the power of the look-alike analysis to isolate the effects of military service on employment conditions of military spouses relies on the quality and completeness of available data. Omitted variable bias occurs when a critical factor influencing employment conditions is missing from the analysis. Although we were able to include in the analysis many characteristics suggested by existing studies as important to employment conditions, some additional factors that may influence these conditions are missing from the census data. For example, as we discussed above, the census data do not contain employers' attitudes toward military and civilian spouses, nor do they show military and civilian spouses' "taste" for work. Therefore, we were unable to adjust for group differences in these characteristics. Consequently, results of statistical analyses of personnel data are best viewed as accurate descriptions of associations among *observable* characteristics of military and civilian spouses and employment conditions.

Policy Implications

The look-alike analysis provides critical information that can help policymakers in making strategic decisions for policy design and implementation. Since the results of the look-alike analysis reveal the extent to which the observable employment disparities can be attributed to observable characteristics (e.g., age, education, mobility, etc.), policymakers can expect to see improvements in narrowing of the gap based on the policy target and design. If a certain policy intervention targets an observable characteristic such as childcare, one can expect to see its effects on employment outcomes with gaps that are at least partly explained by observable characteristics.

The impact of policy aimed at alleviating an unobservable characteristic, such as employer perceptions, is less clear. If employer perceptions are correlated with frequent mobility of military spouses, for instance, policies designed to limit their mobility may also help change employer perceptions, which will in turn be effective in reducing the military-civilian gap. If the observable characteristic, however, is not correlated with any of the unobservable characteristics, unexplained employment disparities will remain intact.

Organization of This Report

This chapter has provided the background, motivation, and a brief discussion of the method for this study, including definitions of variables mentioned in subsequent chapters. The following chapter describes the demographics of military wives using the data from the 2000 population census and compares them with demographics reported in Harrell et al. (2004). Chapter Three explores the employment outcomes of military and civilian wives, as well as the results of the look-alike analysis. These findings are also compared with the findings from the 1990 census. Chapter Four repeats the analysis for military and civilian husbands. Chapter Five discusses the implications of the findings and revisits the recommendations of Harrell et al. (2004).

CHAPTER TWO

Profile of Military Wives

This chapter describes who military wives are and how their characteristics differ from those of their civilian counterparts. We compare military wives' race/ethnicity, age, education, likelihood of having young children at home, geographical mobility, and residential location with those of civilian wives and also with the trends found in the 1990 census.

Racial and Ethnic Profiles of Military and Civilian Wives Have Gotten More Diverse

According to the 2000 census, military wives are more likely to be minority compared with civilian wives. The proportions of minorities among Army and Navy wives are the highest. Air Force (USAF) wives are least likely to be minority among the groups, and their race and ethnicity profile resembles that of civilians the most, with the exception that they are less likely to be Hispanic (see Figure 2.1).

As for specific minority groups, compared with the civilian population, African American wives are overrepresented in almost all services, especially among Army wives. Hispanics are well represented among Army and Marine Corps (USMC) wives, but underrepresented in the Navy and the Air Force groups. Asian American wives are fairly well represented in all service groups, and are overrepresented in the Navy.

Figure 2.1
Race and Ethnicity of Military and Civilian Wives, 1990 and 2000

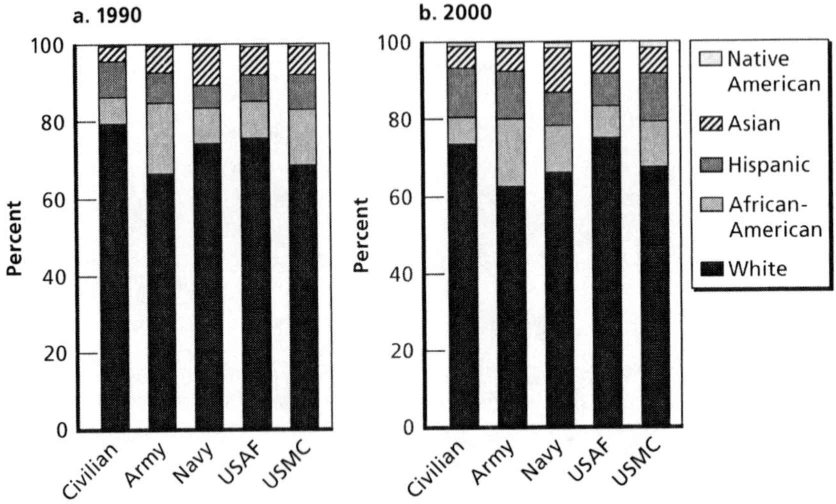

SOURCE: PUMS, 1990 and 2000.
RAND *MG566-2.1*

A notable change in demographic trends since the 1990 census is the expanding proportions of minorities, mostly Hispanic, among military wives. This trend matches the evolving racial profile of civilian wives and reflects the fact that the U.S. population—especially younger Americans—is becoming more racially and ethnically diverse, (Day, 2001).

Although the racial compositions of military and civilian wives share the same trend, wives in the military groups, with the exception of Air Force wives, are still more likely to be minorities. This suggests that race and ethnicity may continue to be a source of employment disparities between the groups. However, both military and civilian wives may now share similar labor market disadvantages associated with being minority women (Higginbotham and Romero, 1997; Browne, 1999).

Military Wives Are More Educated Than Their Civilian Counterparts

The 2000 census data indicate that military wives are more educated than civilian wives. For instance, military wives across all services are more likely than civilian wives to have finished high school (Figure 2.2.b). This finding again contradicts the myth that military wives are less educated than civilian wives (Harrell et al., 2004, p. 15). Among all services, Air Force wives are most likely to be college graduates, while Marine Corps wives are least likely to have completed college. The proportion of military wives who have pursued graduate degrees is similar across all services but smaller than that of civilian wives—possibly reflecting the younger age profile of military wives.

The general trend between the two censuses in educational profiles of civilian and military wives is toward more education. It has become more common to pursue postsecondary education—about seven out of ten military wives across all services have at least some form of college

Figure 2.2
Distribution of Educational Levels of Military and Civilian Wives, 1990 and 2000

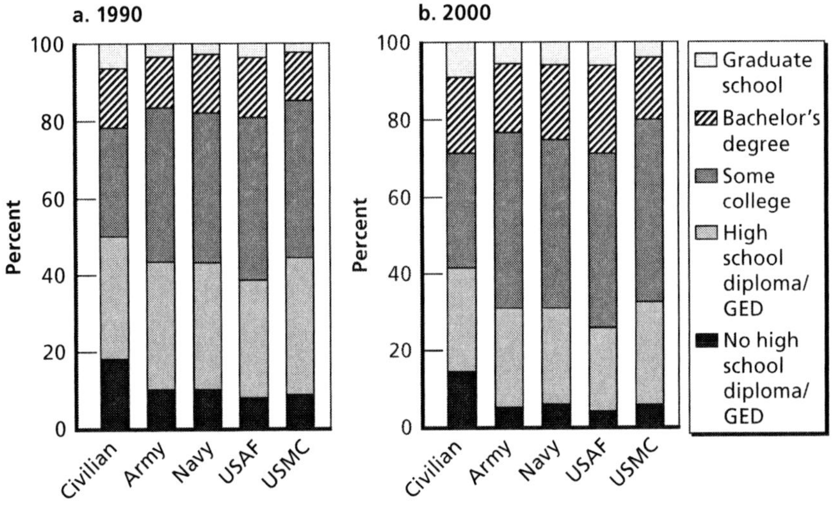

SOURCE: PUMS, 1990 and 2000.
RAND *MG566-2.2*

education or more, whereas the proportion was around six out of ten a decade ago. The trend applies to civilian wives as well—about six out of ten have some college education or more, which is higher than the five out of ten in the previous decade. In these ways, the level of educational attainment can be implicated as a generational factor.

Since education has strong linkages to employment and earnings, this improvement in education may improve the labor market conditions of military wives. However, the universal trend toward more education may reduce the benefits associated with more education for military wives (Pryor and Schafer, 1997; Wolff, 2000). Even so, the relatively higher educational levels of military wives suggest that education is an unlikely source of the employment disparities between civilian and military wives.

Military Wives Are Younger Than Civilian Wives

There is a striking difference in age between civilian and military wives. Military wives are significantly younger than their civilian counterparts: According to the 2000 census, about two-thirds of civilian wives are 44 years old or younger, whereas a similar percentage of Army wives and an even higher percentage of USMC wives are less than 34 years old—at least ten years younger (see Figure 2.3b). On the other end of the spectrum, only about 8 percent of military wives (Army, Navy, and Air Force) are 45 years old or older, whereas 33 percent of civilian wives are in that same age category. The Marine wives are the youngest among the services—only 5 percent are 45 years old or above.

The trends over the last decade indicate that the age profile of civilian wives has changed significantly, whereas the age profile of military wives has changed only marginally. The dramatic changes in the civilian age profile are a result of two demographic trends: aging of the U.S. population (Day, 2001) and delayed marriages among younger people (Lichter and Qian, 2004). These macro-demographic changes have a limited impact on the age profile of military wives because the profile is tied to the structure of the military force and its recruiting and retention.

Figure 2.3
Distribution of Age of Military and Civilian Wives, 1990 and 2000

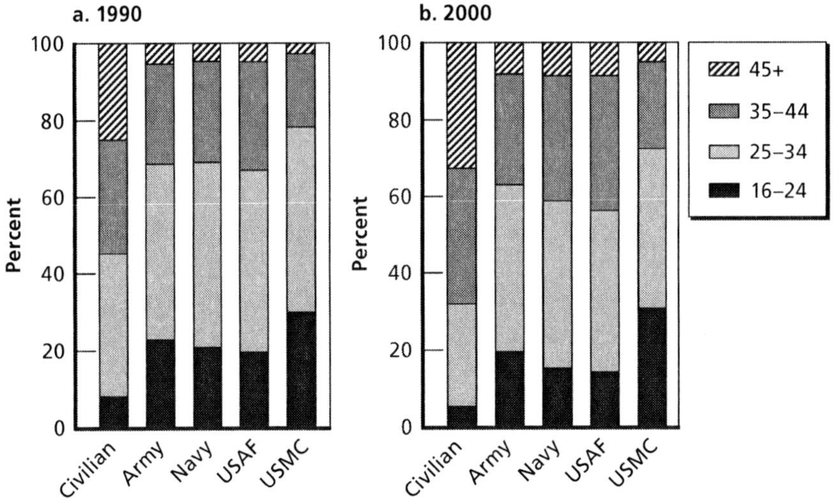

SOURCE: PUMS, 1990 and 2000.
RAND *MG566-2.3*

In 1990, about one in four civilian wives was 45 years old or older; in 2000, that proportion increased to 33 percent. In fact, the proportion of civilian wives in the 16- to 24-year-old age category has declined by one-third since 1990. On the other hand, the trend for the age profiles of military wives is relatively ambiguous. For example, Marine wives are even slightly more likely to be 16 to 24 years old than a decade ago, whereas the proportion of Army, Navy, and Air Force wives who belong to the same age category decreased slightly over the decade. Across services, the proportion in the 35- to 44-year-old age category increased slightly over the decade, and the 45+ category also saw gains on average of about 3 percentage points. Thus, the average age of civilian wives has increased over the past decade, while the age profile of military wives across all services has stayed relatively constant.

The increasing age gap suggests that military wives may face more difficulties in developing their careers, partly because of the complexities associated with being military spouses. Their civilian counterparts are likely to be farther along on their career paths and they may tend to marry later. It remains to be seen how age discrepancy, a fundamental life-cycle factor, contributes to employment opportunities of military wives in the short and long run.

Military Wives Are More Likely to Have Young Children at Home

The 2000 census data suggest that wives in the military group are significantly more likely to have preschool children at home, which is also a factor associated with life cycles. On average, four to five out of ten military wives have at least one young child at home, compared with a mere 29 percent of their civilian counterparts. For specific military services, Army and Marine wives are most likely to have young children, while the Air Force wives are the least likely. However, the differences are subtle, and the percentages of those who have young children at home are quite similar across the military services.

The gap between those who have young children at home and those who do not is now even wider between the two groups. The likelihood for a military wife to have young children at home remained generally constant between 1990 and 2000. In contrast, the chances of civilian wives having preschool children at home decreased by roughly five percentage points from 1990, when about one-third of civilian wives were rearing at least one young child at home.

Such a diverging child-rearing trend suggests that civilian wives might be more advantaged in the job market than their military counterparts because of a much lighter family burden and less responsibility associated with young children. This trend also corresponds to the fact that military wives are significantly younger and are more likely to be in the stage of developing their skill sets and career paths. The combined effect of child rearing, as a competing demand from work, and being at an early stage in career development may explain the lower income levels and employment rates associated with military wives (Figure 2.4).

Figure 2.4
Civilian and Military Wives Who Have a Young Child at Home, 1990 and 2000

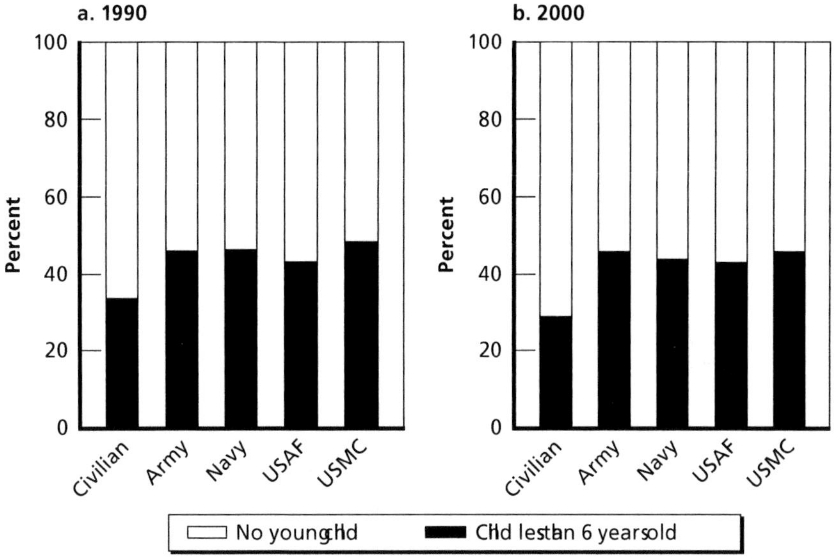

SOURCE: PUMS, 1990 and 2000.
RAND *MG566-2.4*

Military Families Move Farther and More Frequently Than Civilians

According to the 2000 census, there is still a drastic difference in residence mobility between military and civilian wives (Figure 2.5.b). More than half of the civilian wives had not moved for the past five years, and among those who moved, most moved within the same state. In contrast, only about 10 percent of military wives stayed at the same home for the past five years, and most moved to a different state. Out-of-state moves are much less likely for their civilian counterparts. In general, military wives are also more likely to move abroad.

As for specific services, Marine wives were the most likely to have moved during the past five years, while Navy wives were the least likely.

Figure 2.5
Geographical Mobility of Military and Civilian Wives, 1990 and 2000

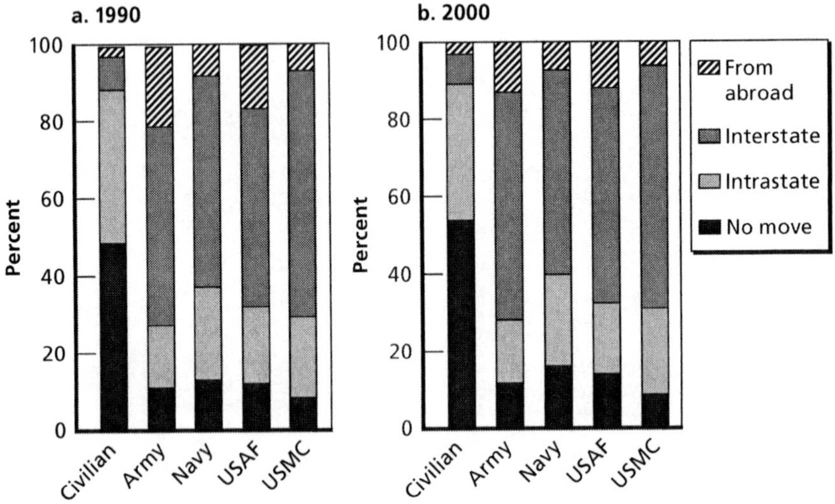

SOURCE: PUMS, 1990 and 2000.
RAND *MG566-2.5*

Among all military services, Army and Air Force wives are more likely to move to or from abroad than are Navy and Marine Corps wives.

Compared with a decade before, both military and civilian wives are slightly more likely to stay at the same residence for the past five years. However, the notable gap in the extent of mobility remains the same—military wives are still much more likely to move farther or more frequently than their civilian counterparts in both 1990 and 2000. Although the general gap in mobility between civilian and military wives has been constant, trends differ slightly among the military services. For example, one in five Army wives had moved to or from abroad during the past five years in 1990, while the proportion was reduced to one in eight in 2000. Air Force wives also tended to move abroad less in 2000 than in 1990. Mobility patterns for Navy and Marine wives have remained relatively constant.

Geographical mobility might result in an unstable social network for military wives, whereas a stable network may be key to getting a decent job. Also, military wives' frequent long-distance moves may increase their employers' reluctance to offer long-term on-the-job training. Since military wives are constantly on the move over the years, geographical mobility may continue to be associated with the income and employment differences of wives between the two groups.

Military Wives Are Still More Likely to Live in Metropolitan Areas

According to the 2000 census, more than eight out of ten wives live in metropolitan areas, and military wives are more likely to be living in metropolitan areas than their civilian counterparts. Among all military services, Navy wives are the most urbanized, with only 5 percent of them living in nonmetropolitan areas. Army wives are least likely to live in metropolitan areas, which matches the location pattern of civilian wives (Figure 2.6).

Figure 2.6
Percentage of Military and Civilian Wives Living in Metropolitan Areas, 1990 and 2000

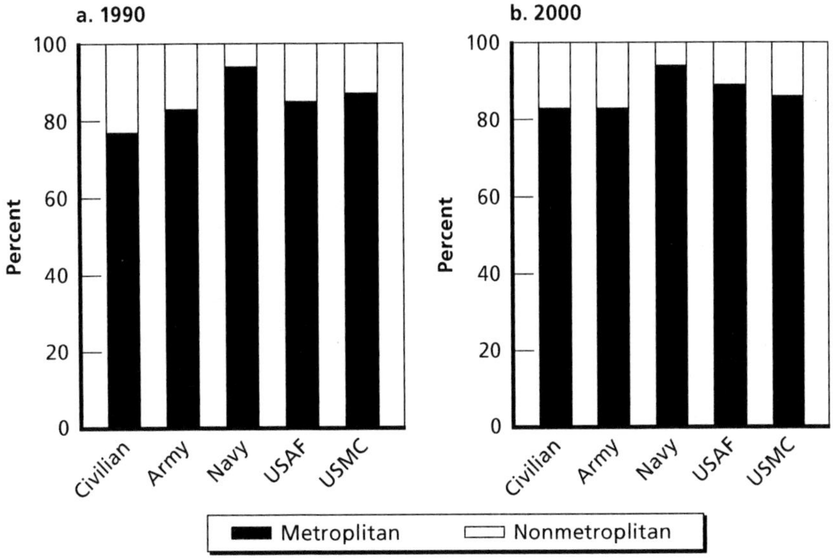

SOURCE: PUMS, 1990 and 2000.

RAND *MG566-2.6*

According to the 2000 census, six percentage points more civilian wives are living in metropolitan areas than a decade before. However, military wives do not seem to follow this upward trend. Across all military services, the percentage living in metropolitan areas has remained rather constant. Air Force wives are only marginally more inclined to be living in a metropolitan area, while the likelihood for USMC wives decreased by one percentage point from 1990.

The trend is toward a smaller difference between civilian and military wives with respect to whether or not they live in a metropolitan area. Empirically, metropolitan areas are usually associated with more job opportunities and higher pay. This factor alone would thus be expected to shrink the employment disparities favoring civilian wives.

We revisit this expectation in Chapter Three, when we compare the income levels of military and civilian wives while controlling for geographic location.

Summary

In this chapter we described military and civilian wives in 2000 and compared them with military and civilian wives of a decade ago. Military wives are more racially and ethnically diverse than civilian wives, and they are well-educated—often having reached a higher educational level than civilian wives. They also tend to be younger than civilian wives and are more likely to be rearing young children. Thus, military wives appear to be at a different stage in their life cycles than are civilian wives. Military life-style demands also appear to set military wives apart from civilian wives. Military wives are much more likely to relocate than are their civilian counterparts and to live near metropolitan areas, which contradicts the perception that they live in rural and remote areas where military bases tend to be located.

For a few of these factors, trends have either been flat since 1990 or have moved similarly for civilian and military wives. However, the age gap between military and civilian wives is wider in 2000 than it was in 1990; the likelihood of having a young child at home has been decreasing for civilian wives while remaining the same for military wives; and the probability of living in a metropolitan area for civilian wives is increasing to resemble that of military wives. Although these observable differences in demographic, life-cycle, and military life-style factors and the corresponding trends over time imply generally unfavorable employment outcomes for military wives, more analysis is needed to determine how significant the disparities are when we control for differences in background characteristics.

In the next chapter, we describe the relationships between employment status and earnings of military and civilian wives. We also analyze the extent to which the disparities may be explained by the differences we have described in this chapter.

CHAPTER THREE

Military and Civilian Wives' Employment Conditions

The previous chapter provided an update on demographic trends for military and civilian wives using data from the latest census. This chapter describes the employment conditions of military wives in 2000 and how they may have changed from the previous decade.

Military Wives Are Less Likely to Be Employed

Here we continue to use the definitions of labor force, employment, and unemployment that Harrell et al. (2004) used: The labor force is made up of individuals who are either employed or jobless but actively looking for work (unemployed). Individuals who are not employed and are not actively looking for work are not considered to be part of the labor force. Therefore, there are two kinds of jobless people: those who are unemployed (and thus actively seeking work) and those who are not part of the labor force (and thus not seeking work). In the look-alike analyses, the population consists of both those who are in and out of the labor force, in order to accurately estimate the look-alike comparison groups. Thus, the calculations of employment and unemployment rates in this report are based on the total population and not just those who are in the labor force.[1]

[1] Figure 3.1 is an exception. It follows the U.S. government's estimations of the unemployment rate, which is based on the labor force.

Figure 3.1.b shows that, according to the 2000 census, military wives are more likely to opt out of the labor force than are their civilian counterparts. Among military wives who are in the labor force, there appears to be a greater probability of unemployment compared with civilian wives, who are almost 97 percent employed.[2] Thus, although employment prospects are very good for both groups, civilian wives are more likely to find employment than military wives. Across services, Air Force and Navy wives are slightly more likely to be employed, and Army and Marine wives are slightly more likely to be seeking work. Figure 3.1.a reveals a similar distribution in the 1990 census data.

A more in-depth look at the wives' employment patterns confirms the difference between military and civilian wives. In Figure 3.2, we

Figure 3.1
Employment Status of Civilian and Military Wives, 1990 and 2000

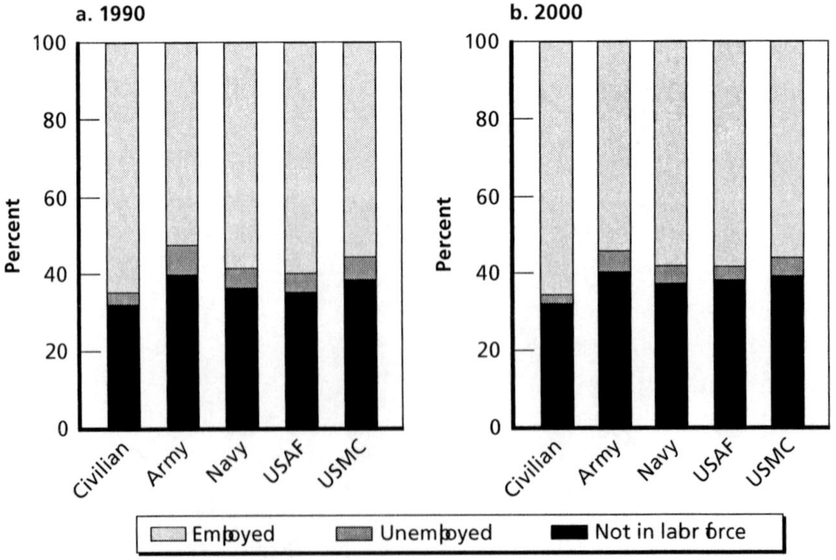

SOURCE: PUMS, 1990 and 2000.
RAND *MG566-3.1*

---

2 According to the 2000 census, 67.79 percent of civilian wives are in the labor force and 65.44 percent are employed. 65.44 percent divided by 67.79 percent yields an employment rate of 97 percent (employed/labor force).

Figure 3.2
Percentage Employed Among Civilian, Military, and Look-Alike Civilian Wives, 1990 and 2000

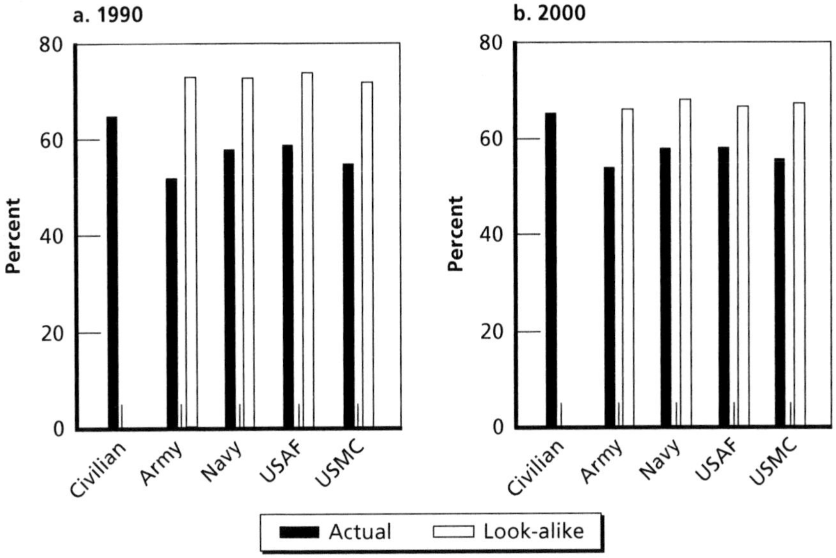

RAND *MG566-3.2*

compare military wives with civilian wives who share the same observable characteristics, (as before, we refer to them as "look-alikes" by using the propensity score analysis.[3] The second bar for each military service illustrates employment rates for civilian wives who share the same observable characteristics (e.g., age, education, and location) as the military wives. Because the employment rates of military wives are substantially less than those of their civilian look-alike counterparts, we infer that having a military spouse may adversely affect the labor market outlook for the wife. The magnitude of the difference is similar across services, except for the Air Force, which exhibits slightly less discrepancy. The differences between the rates for military wives and look-alike civilians are actually slightly larger than those between the rates for military wives and all civilian wives. Thus, observable characteristics alone suggest that military wives should have slightly *higher*

[3] Results of the propensity score analysis are in Tables A.1a–A.1.d in the appendix.

employment rates than average civilian wives. Unobservable factors might be pushing the military-wife employment rates down to the levels actually measured.

In comparing the results of 2000 census data with the results of 1990 census data in Figure 3.2, one can see that the differences between military wives and their look-alikes—that is, the employment rate differences that can be attributed to unobservable factors—have decreased. Also, those civilian wives who look like military wives have employment rates that are not as far above those for the whole civilian wife population as they were a decade before.

Military Spouses Are More Likely Than Civilians to Be Unemployed

Among those who are in the labor force, the 2000 census indicates that military wives, especially those who are married to Army and Marine servicemen, are more likely to be unemployed (see Figure 3.3.b). This marked difference may be attributable to where the two groups are in their respective stages in life. For instance, more-recent college graduates are likely to be seeking work, whereas women near retirement age may opt out of the labor force once they are out of jobs.

The past decade has seen unemployment rates decline across the board for those seeking work, and that trend is observed in both the military wives and their civilian counterparts (Figure 3.3). A greater decrease in unemployment rates is seen for military wives, especially Army wives. In 1990, 13 percent of Army wives were unemployed and seeking work. By 2000, that figure had dropped to 9 percent, or less than one in ten Army wives. But the unemployment gap between civilian and military wives remains, even though a more robust economy would be expected to improve the employment prospects of the unemployed in particular (Martel and Kelter, 2000). This seeming employment disadvantage for military wives suggests that recent policies and programs implemented to address this issue may have been efficacious to some degree but have been insufficient to make employment opportunities equitable for military wives.

Figure 3.3
Unemployment Rate (Percentage Seeking Work) Among Civilian and Military Wives, 1990 and 2000

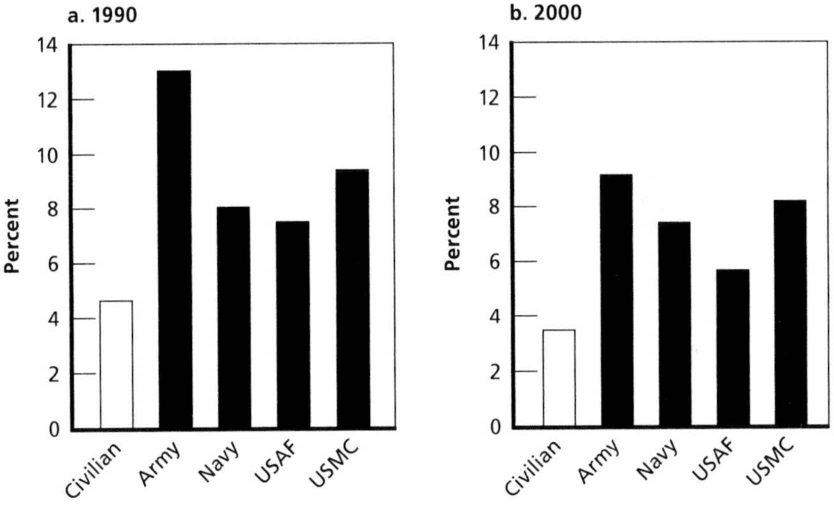

SOURCE: PUMS, 1990 and 2000.
RAND *MG566-3.3*

Again, the look-alike analysis can shed light on these apparent relationships. For all military services, the second bar of each pair in Figure 3.4 indicates that the civilian look-alikes have less unemployment than their military counterparts. This difference is most striking for Army wives and their look-alikes. In contrast, the unemployment rate for Air Force wives closely resembles that of civilians who look like Air Force wives. The difference in unemployment rates between Air Force wives and civilian wives in general, therefore, is mostly due to observable characteristics. Policy interventions based on observable characteristics are likely to be able to significantly reduce the gap. But overall, Figure 3.4 supports the notion that there are unobservable factors leading to the different unemployment rates between civilian and military wives; civilian wives who look like military wives have higher unemployment rates than civilian wives.

Figure 3.4
Percentage Unemployed Among Civilian, Military, and Look-Alike Civilian Wives, 1990 and 2000

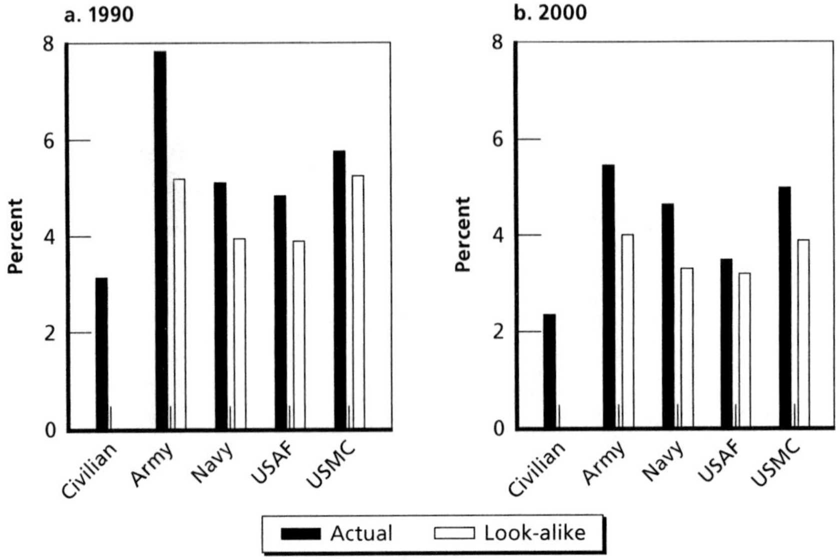

SOURCE: PUMS, 1990 and 2000.
RAND *MG566-3.4*

The findings of this analysis depart slightly from a similar analysis performed using the 1990 census data. The gaps in the unemployment rates of Army and Air Force wives and their look-alike civilian counterparts are smaller in 2000 than they were a decade ago, suggesting either that the observable characteristics are factoring more into the story, or that the unobserved characteristics are having less of an effect than before.

Military Wives Earn Less Than Civilian Wives

A comparison of hourly wages of military and civilian wives from the 2000 census shows that, on average, across all services, the civilian wives are paid more per hour than military wives (see Figure 3.5.b). Civilian wives earn, on average, almost $12 an hour, whereas military wives tend to earn an average hourly wage of about $9. Among the

Figure 3.5
Hourly Wages of Civilian and Military Wives, 1990 and 2000

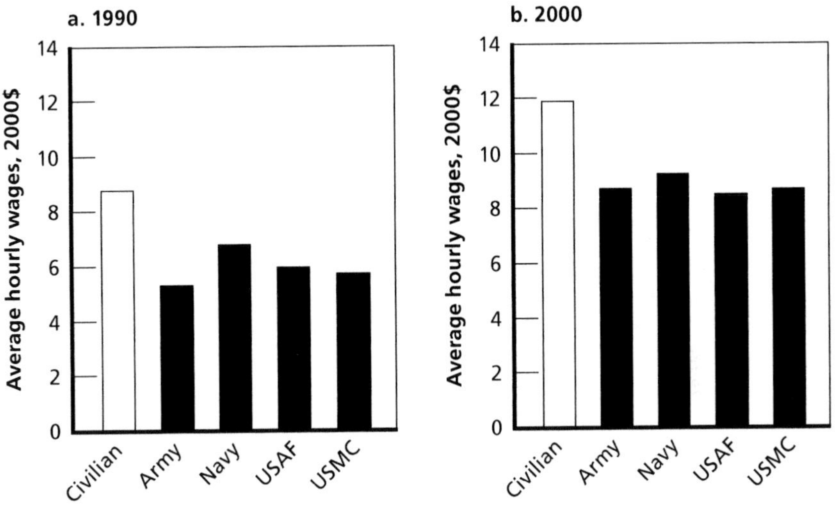

SOURCE: PUMS, 1990 and 2000.
RAND *MG566-3.5*

services, Navy wives are paid slightly more than wives of other servicemen; and Air Force wives receive the lowest average hourly wages.

Compared with the hourly wages in 1990 illustrated in Figure 3.5.a, wages (adjusted for inflation) are higher across the board in 2000, and the wage differences across military services, especially between the Army and the Marine wives, have become less sharp.

Figure 3.6 compares the actual hourly wages with the wages of look-alikes of military wives. It illustrates that, with the same observable profiles, the wives of military men should be earning higher wages. However, according to the 2000 census, the look-alike wages are slightly lower than the wages of civilian wives. The opposite was true in 1990; the wages of look-alike civilian wives were higher than the average wages of civilian wives. This suggests that, in 2000, based only on observable profiles—e.g., education, age, and location of residence—military wives are no longer more advantaged than civilian wives in terms of what their wages would be if they were not married to military men.

Figure 3.6
Hourly Wages Among Civilian, Military, and Look-Alike Civilian Wives, 1990 and 2000

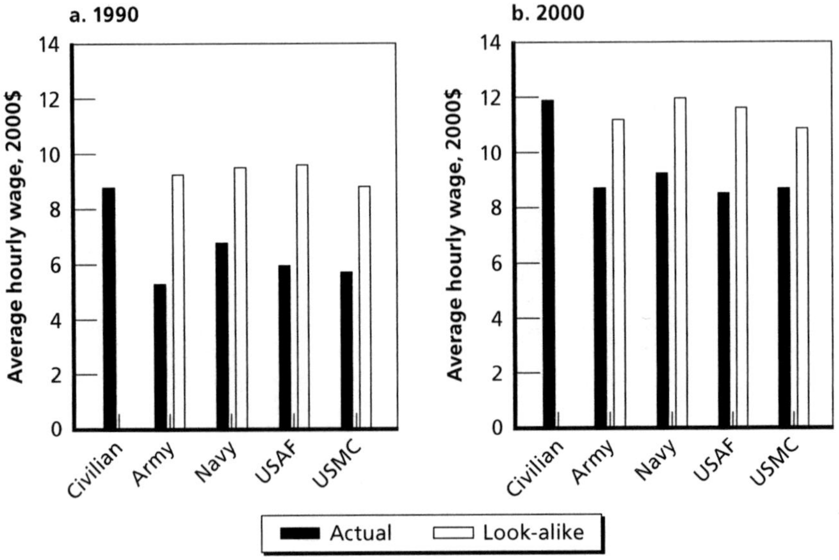

SOURCE: PUMS, 1990 and 2000.
RAND *MG566-3.6*

The wage differences may be associated with the difference in age distribution between civilian and military wives. Military wives tend to be much younger, so there should be a higher percentage of younger military wives joining the workforce as the older wives retire or opt out of the labor force for various reasons. It is reasonable to assume that these young wives earn lower wages than older wives who have more-developed skill sets and are farther along on their career path. However, the look-alike civilians, whose ages are similar to those of the military wives, should then have wage rates similar to those of the military wives, when instead they are more similar to those of civilian wives in general. Indeed, the results of the look-alike analysis suggest that most of the differences between military and civilian wives' hourly wages cannot be explained by observable characteristics.

Relative Earnings of Military Wives Living in Metropolitan Areas

National earnings comparisons might be biased if military wives tended to live in areas with lower (or higher) wages. Furthermore, local labor market conditions give significance to the wage rates since the wage structure and cost of living differ by locale. A military wife's wage, for example, may be considered fairly high in an area where other wages (and, most likely, the cost of living) are low, whereas in another area (quite likely with a higher cost of living), the same wage might be at the bottom of the wage scale. We therefore compared military and civilian wives who live in the same metropolitan statistical areas (MSAs).

This comparison does not isolate the net effect of being a military spouse on one's relative earning when observed characteristics are controlled for, as the look-alike analysis did in the previous section. Instead, it aims to describe military spouses' relative earnings compared with civilians living in the same labor market.

To accomplish this goal, we first grouped all residents of each MSA into ten equal groups, or deciles, based on their hourly wages. For instance, the first group has the lowest wage earners, while the tenth group belongs to the highest wage earners within a MSA. Then we assigned each wife to a decile group based on her annual wage. Finally, we combined the results by decile across metropolitan areas. Thus, if the wages of military and civilian wives have identical distributions, we would see them as overlapping lines in Figure 3.7.

As can be seen in Figure 3.7, military wives are underrepresented (less than 10 percent) among the high-wage deciles and overrepresented (more than 10 percent) among the low-wage deciles, while the civilian wives appear to be approximately evenly represented in each decile, with a slight overrepresentation in the middle deciles. About half of military wives across all services belong to the bottom 40 percent of wage earnings, and only a small fraction are at the higher end. For civilian wives, the distribution was more even, with about 41 percent belonging to the bottom four decile groups and 37 percent belonging to the top four deciles. Among the services, Marine wives appear to be

Figure 3.7
Military Wives' Earnings, by Service, Compared with Those of Civilian Wives Living in the Same MSA, 1990 and 2000

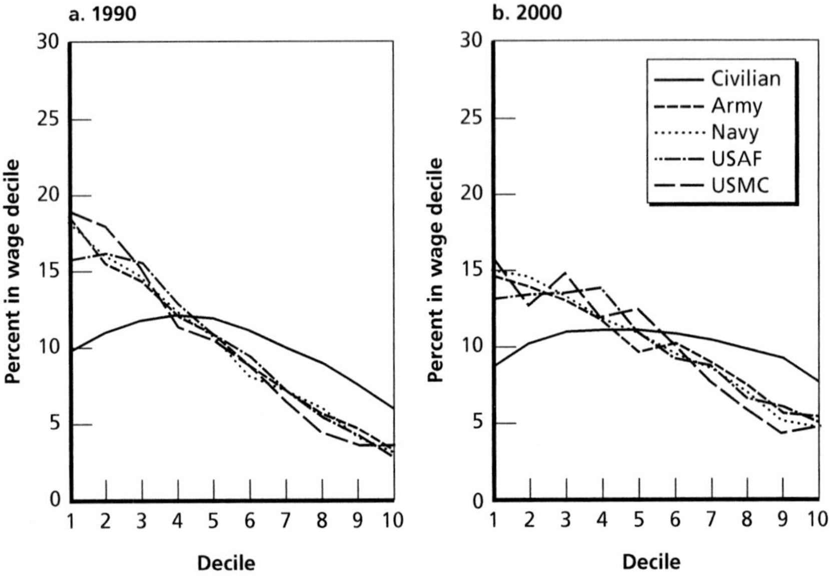

SOURCE: PUMS, 1990 and 2000.
RAND *MG566-3.7*

worst off; they are most likely to be overrepresented in the low-wage deciles and most likely to be underrepresented in the high-wage deciles.

In comparison with 1990, the disparities in income positions appear to be smaller for both military and civilian wives. Military wives are less likely to be overrepresented in the first decile of low-wage earners, and less likely to be underrepresented in the tenth decile of high-wage earners. The distribution of civilian wives across deciles is more even than it was a decade before as well.

Figure 3.8 compares percentages of civilian and military wives in the same wage deciles, for those with less than a high school education in both 1990 and 2000. Accounting for educational attainment in the metropolitan-level analysis produces more accurate comparisons of military and civilian wives' wages because wages are often positively

Figure 3.8
Earnings of Military Wives Without a High School Diploma, by Service, Compared with Those of Civilian Wives, 1990 and 2000

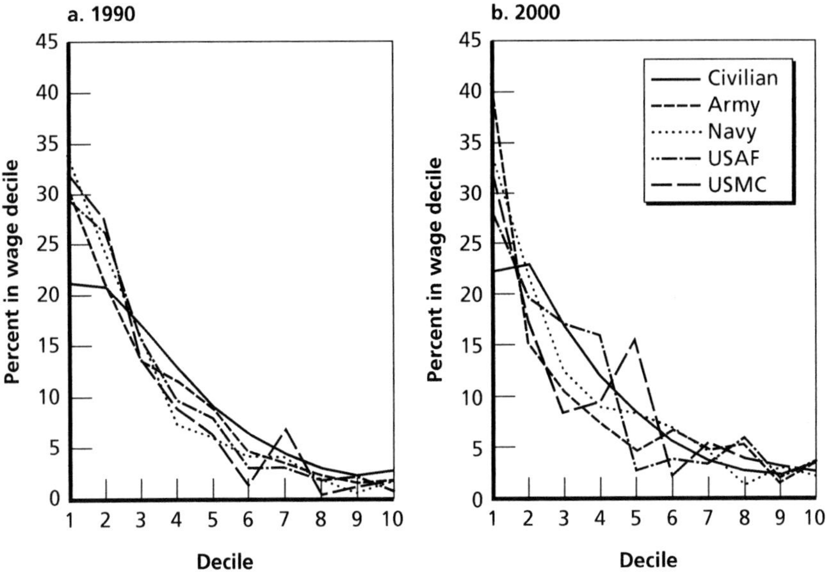

SOURCE: PUMS, 1990 and 2000.
RAND *MG566-3.8*

associated with education. Noticeably, military wives with no high school diploma are much more likely than civilian wives to earn the lowest hourly wages. In 1990, about 30–35 percent of military wives across all services belonged to the lowest wage decile, whereas only about 21 percent of civilian wives were in the same category. This discrepancy has not change substantially in the ten years since. Slightly more wives, both civilian and military, are at the high end of wage rates, but the general distribution of hourly wages earned by civilian wives has not been significantly changed, and military wives of the same education level still seem to be worse off in the job market. However, it appears that Marine wives are more inclined to earn a mid-range hourly wage than wives married to other servicemen.

Figure 3.9 shows the percentages in each wage decile, according to the 1990 and 2000 censuses, for civilian and military wives who

Figure 3.9
Earnings of Military Wives with a High School Diploma or GED, by Service, Compared with Those of Civilian Wives, 1990 and 2000

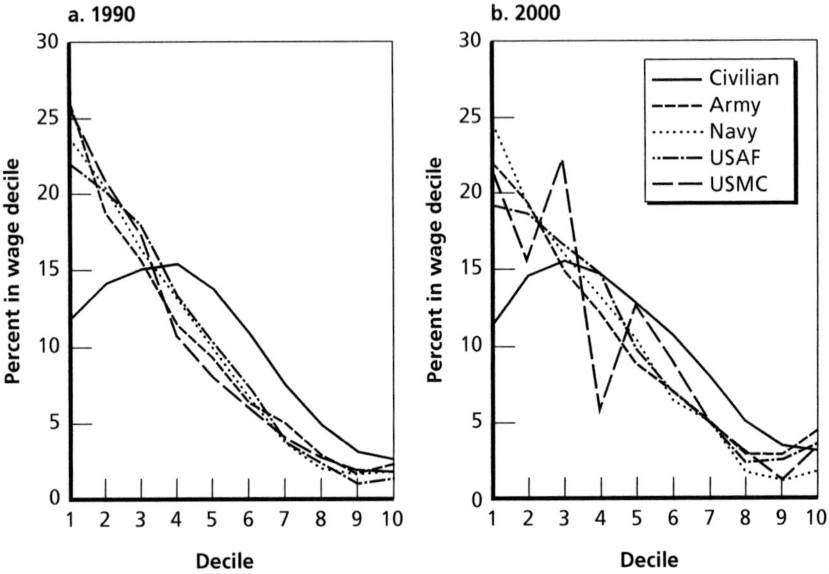

SOURCE: PUMS, 1990 and 2000.
RAND *MG566-3.9*

acquired a high school diploma or equivalent. It indicates that, compared with 1990 data, both civilian and military wives with only a high school diploma or equivalent are doing slightly better in the job market in 2000. Nonetheless, civilian-military differences remain.

Figure 3.10 compares wage positions, according to the 1990 and 2000 censuses, of civilian and military wives with some college education. Like wives who have less education, civilian wives with some years in college generally receive a higher wage rate than their military counterparts. It seems that the wages of Marine wives are more likely to be in the lowest wage decile than wives of other military services, let alone the civilian wives. The wage positions of both civilian and military wives did not change significantly from 1990 to 2000.

Figure 3.10
Earnings of Military Wives with Some College, by Service, Compared with Those of Civilian Wives, 1990 and 2000

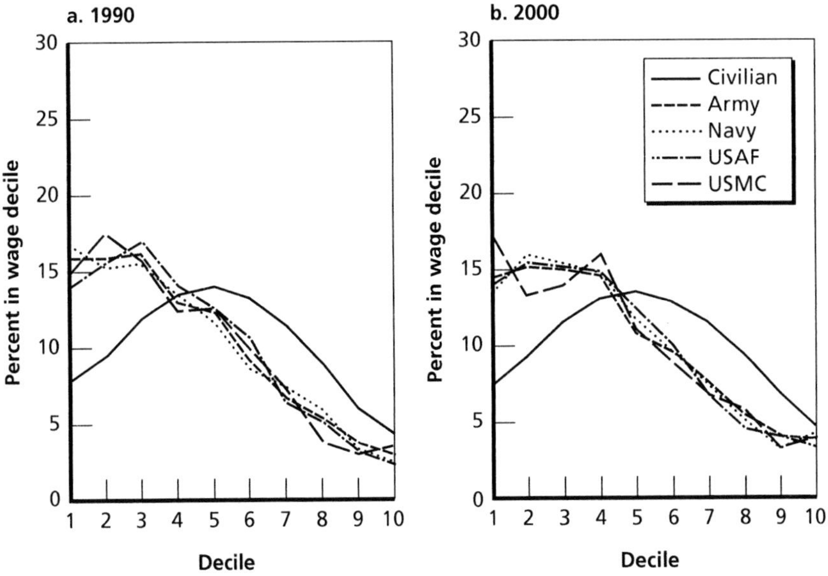

SOURCE: PUMS, 1990 and 2000.
RAND *MG566-3.10*

Figure 3.11 compares wage positions of civilian and military wives who obtained bachelor's degrees, according to the 1990 and 2000 censuses. Unlike wives who have less education, military wives with bachelor's degrees are more likely to earn mid-range wages than their civilian counterparts. Among all services, in 2000, Army and Navy wives are doing better at the higher end of the wage deciles. In contrast, Marine wives seem to be worse off than other wives. The wage positions of civilian wives did not change significantly from 1990 to 2000, but there has been a small improvement in the wage profiles for military wives. Military wives are less likely to be earning low wages in 2000.

Figure 3.11
Earnings of Military Wives with a Bachelor's Degree, by Service, Compared with Those of Civilian Wives, 1990 and 2000

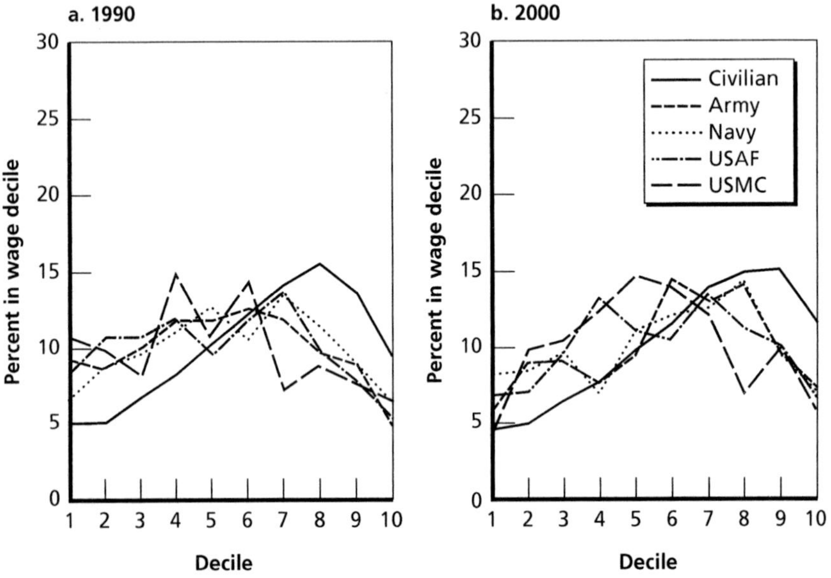

SOURCE: PUMS, 1990 and 2000.
RAND *MG566-3.11*

Summary

In this chapter, we have compared employment status and earnings of military and civilian wives. We found that, according to 2000 census data, military wives are less likely to be employed than civilian wives and are more likely to be unemployed. Military wives also earn less than civilian wives.

Of the military wives, Navy wives are the most likely to be in the labor force and also earn the most. However, with the exception of a substantially lower unemployment rate for Air Force wives than for those married to other servicemen, differences among the services are generally small. None of the individual service outcomes is as favorable as that for civilians.

We also compared the employment outcomes of 2000 with those of 1990. Labor force participation rates are similar between 1990 and 2000 for both civilian and military wives. Unemployment rates, however, have fallen substantially for all wives, particularly for Army wives, who had the highest rates. Hourly wages (unadjusted for inflation) are up for both civilian wives and wives across the military services.

We sought to determine the extent to which differences in civilian and military wives' employment conditions in 2000 might be explained by the differences in potentially relevant background factors described in Chapter Two. To do so, we performed the look-alike (propensity score) analysis to create a sample of civilian wives who are similar to the wives affiliated with each service regarding the factors reported in Chapter Two.

Overall, the look-alike civilian wives have similar employment rates and wages to the civilian wives. The background factors we considered thus do not explain much of the difference between civilian and military wives; most of the difference in employment rates must be due to unobserved factors, which might include differing tastes for work or possible bias by employers. However, observed background differences explain about 70 percent of the difference in unemployment rate between civilian and Navy and Army wives and about 80 percent of the difference between civilian wives and Marine Corps wives.

National earnings comparisons might be biased if military wives tended to live in areas with lower (or higher) wages. We therefore compared civilian and military wives according to where they fell across the overall wage-earning distribution for each metropolitan statistical area and aggregated the results.[4] The results are consistent with the national-level data: Military wives are more likely than civilian wives to fall in the bottom 30 percent of the distribution of all wage-earners and less likely to fall in the top 40 percent. However, as in the national data, military wives have gained a little on civilian wives since 1990. Differences across services are small, but Army wives appear to have

---

4 This analysis is intended to demonstrate the relative earnings of military wives compared with civilian wives within the same metropolitan area and is not part of the propensity score (look-alike) analysis.

a slightly more favorable earnings distribution than the others, and Marine Corps wives have a slightly less favorable one.

We repeated the metropolitan-level analysis for different levels of education, from those with no high school diploma to those with a bachelor's degree. For wives of equivalent education, military wives were again more likely than civilian wives to be near the lower end of the wage distribution and less likely to be toward the higher end.

CHAPTER FOUR

Profile of Military Husbands

The 2000 census data afford us an opportunity to learn about the husbands of women who are serving in the military. In investigating military husbands' characteristics and employment conditions, we aggregated data for military husbands across all services into a single "military" category because of the small sample size.

Military Husbands Are Less Likely to Be White

Figure 4.1 shows that military husbands are less likely to be white. The number of whites among civilian husbands approaches 80 percent, while only 60 percent of military husbands are white. Noticeably, military African American husbands are over-represented—military husbands are three time more likely to be African Americans than are civilian husbands; almost three out of ten military husbands are African American. On the other hand, it appears that Hispanics and Asians are relatively underrepresented in the military group compared with their percentages among the civilian population.

Military Husbands Are More Educated Than Civilian Counterparts

Figure 4.2 compares the educational profiles of civilian and military husbands. Military husbands tend to be more educated in general—

Figure 4.1
Race and Ethnicity of Military and Civilian Husbands

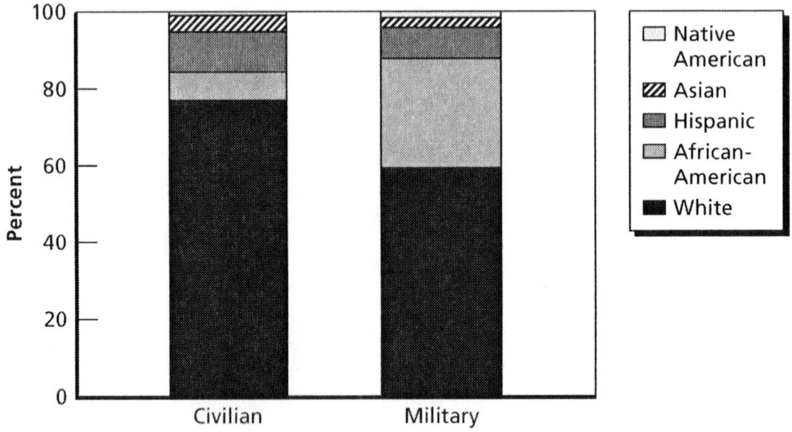

SOURCE: PUMS 2000.
RAND *MG566-4.1*

Figure 4.2
Distribution of Educational Levels of Military and Civilian Husbands

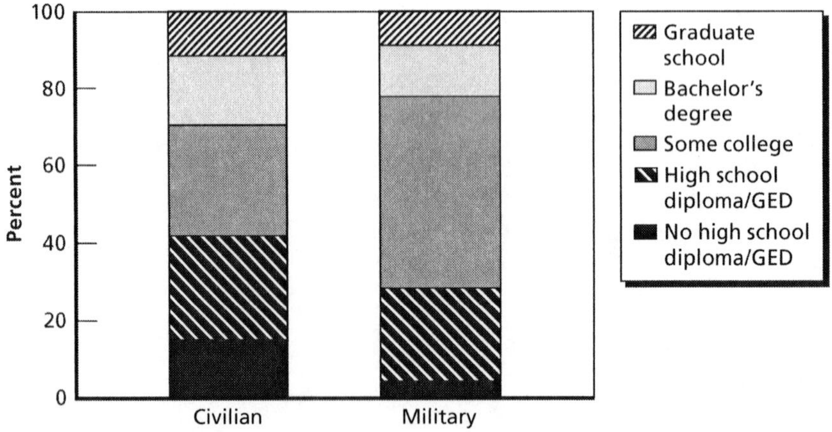

SOURCE: PUMS 2000.
RAND *MG566-4.2*

almost all military husbands (around 96 percent) have at least completed high school, while only 85 percent of civilian husbands have done so. This finding reflects the demographic trend that Americans tend to marry those with similar educational attainment (Mare, 1991). As Harrell et al. (2004, pp. 15–16) point out, a high school diploma is generally a minimum requirement for entry into the military. Thus, just as military women are more likely to be more educated than their civilian counterparts, so are their husbands.

However, civilian husbands are more likely to have obtained a bachelor's degree or to have pursued advanced studies than have military husbands. This is reflected by the fact that about 50 percent of all military husbands have some college education but have not graduated from college with a degree. In contrast, only 30 percent of civilian husbands are in the same category

The fact that 50 percent of military husbands are attending or have attended some college but have not obtained a bachelor's degree could imply that (1) military husbands tend to be younger than their civilian counterparts and thus are more likely to be in the midst of attending college, or (2) frequent and long-distance moves associated with their wives' military services (see below) are disrupting their college education.

Military Husbands Are More Likely to Have Young Children at Home

Figure 4.3 illustrates the percentage of husbands who have at least one child (in the household) who is less than six years old. Husbands who have or do not have young children at home may have older children, but young children at home are of interest here because they demand more time and care from parents. It is notable that military husbands are more likely to have at least one preschool child at home. Forty percent of military husbands have one or more preschool children, compared with merely 25 percent of civilian husbands in the same category.

Figure 4.3
Military and Civilian Husbands Who Have a Young Child at Home

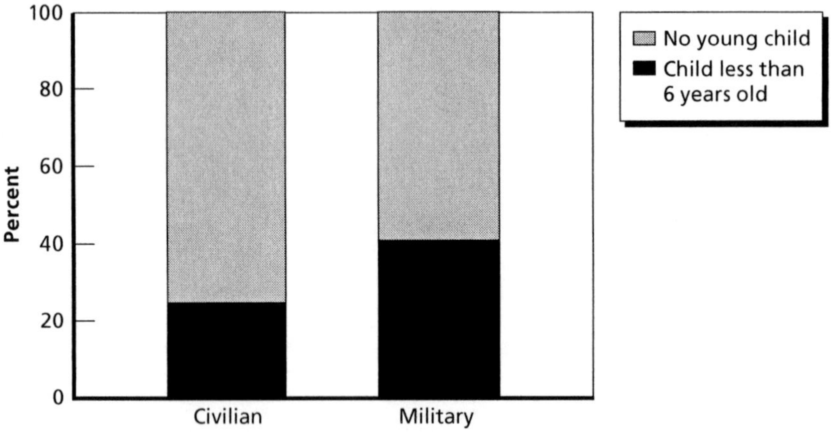

SOURCE: PUMS 2000.
RAND *MG566-4.3*

Military Husbands Move Farther and More Frequently Than Civilian Husbands

Figure 4.4 indicates different degrees of geographic mobility between civilian and military husbands. According to the 2000 census, military husbands relocate farther and more often than civilian husbands do. More than 50 percent of civilian husbands have not changed their place of residence for the past five years, whereas fewer than 20 percent of military husbands are in the same category. Among husbands who do move, military husbands also tend to make more interstate moves than their civilian counterparts. In fact, 50 percent of all military husbands moved across states during the past five years, while only about 8 percent of civilian husbands moved that far away. Most civilian husbands who did move relocated within the same state. Also, civilian husbands are very unlikely to move across countries—only one in 50 did so for the past five years, compared with one in ten military husbands.

Figure 4.4
Geographical Mobility of Military and Civilian Husbands During the Five Years Prior to the 2000 Census

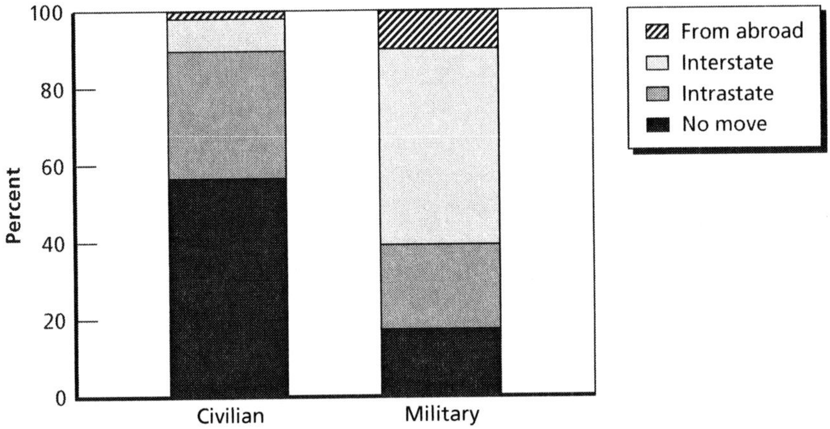

SOURCE: PUMS 2000.
RAND *MG566-4.4*

Employment Status of Military Husbands Differs from Employment Status of Civilian Husbands

Figure 4.5 depicts the employment status of military and civilian husbands. We use the same definitions here for labor force as we did in the previous chapter: The labor force includes individuals who are employed and unemployed (i.e., those who are jobless but actively seeking work); individuals who are not employed and not looking for work are not in the labor force. Again, the calculations of employment and unemployment rates are based on the population and not just on those who are in the labor force. The left bar shows the employment status of civilian husbands; the other two bars show that of military husbands and their look-alike civilian husbands.[1]

---

1 Table 1.2 lists the variables that were included in the propensity score (look-alike) analysis. Results of the propensity score analysis are in Table A.3 in the appendix.

Figure 4.5
Employment Status of Civilian, Military, and Look-Alike Civilian Husbands

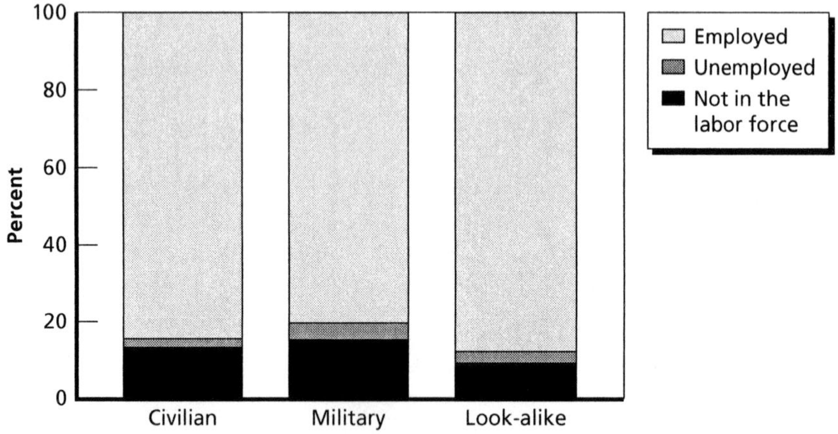

SOURCE: PUMS 2000.
RAND *MG566-4.5*

Military husbands are slightly less likely to be in the labor force than their civilian counterparts and to have a job. Among those who are actively looking for a job, military husbands also have a higher likelihood of being unemployed than their civilian counterparts.

However, the third bar suggests that the civilian husbands whose observable characteristics resemble those of military husbands are more likely to be in the labor force and more likely to have a job than both military and civilian husbands. This suggests that there might be some unobservable factors that account for military husbands' disadvantage in the job market.

Military Husbands Are More Likely to Be Unemployed Than Civilian Husbands

Figure 4.6 shows that the percentage of unemployed military husbands is twice as high as that of unemployed civilian husbands. Civilian husbands whose observable characters are similar to those of military husbands are less likely to be unemployed than military husbands. However,

Figure 4.6
Percentage Unemployed Among Civilian, Military, and Look-Alike Civilian Husbands

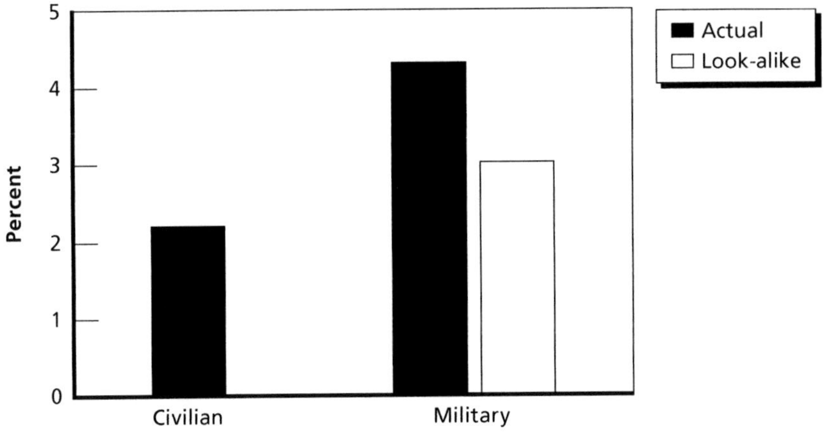

SOURCE: PUMS 2000.
RAND *MG566-4.6*

this rate is still about one percentage point higher than that of civilian husbands, suggesting that both observable and unobservable characteristic differences contribute to the unemployment rate gap.

Military Husbands Earn Less Than Civilian Husbands

In Figure 4.7, the left-most bar represents the average annual income of civilian husbands, and the other two bars show the average annual income of military husbands and that of civilian husbands who look like their military counterparts. Civilian husbands earn on average above $40,000 every year, whereas military husbands earn significantly less—roughly $30,000 annually. The look-alike civilian husbands would earn a higher annual wage than military husbands do but would still earn less than a typical civilian husband.

These findings suggest that both observed and unobserved characteristics of husbands contribute to their annual income differences;

Figure 4.7
Annual Income of Civilian, Military, and Look-Alike Civilian Husbands

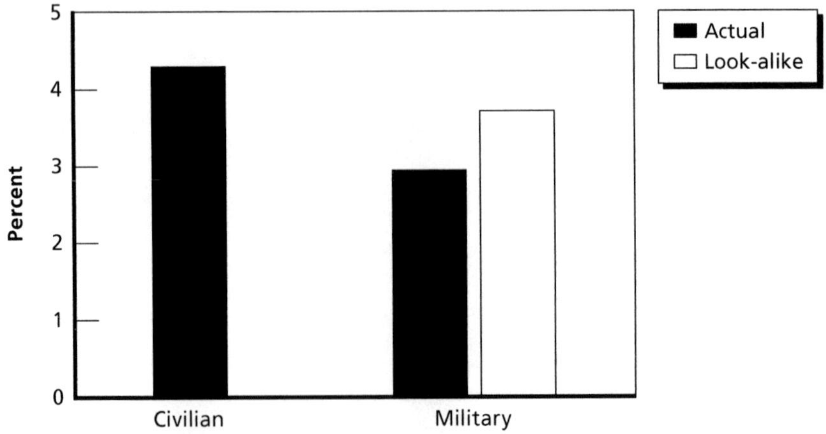

SOURCE: PUMS 2000.
RAND *MG566-4.7*

more of the gap is explained by unobserved characteristics than by observed characteristics.

Similarly in Figure 4.8, the left-most bar represents the average hourly wage rate of civilian husbands, and the two other show the average hourly wage rate of military husbands and that of civilian husbands who look like their military counterparts.

The figure again proves that civilian husbands are better off in terms of income. Civilian husbands' wage rate is about $21 per hour, whereas military husbands earn only $17 an hour. The look-alike civilian husbands' wage rate is slightly higher than that of military husbands—raising their would-be average by $1 per hour. Still, it is significantly lower than that of civilian husbands on average.

Figure 4.8
Hourly Wages Among Civilian, Military, and Look-Alike Civilian Husbands

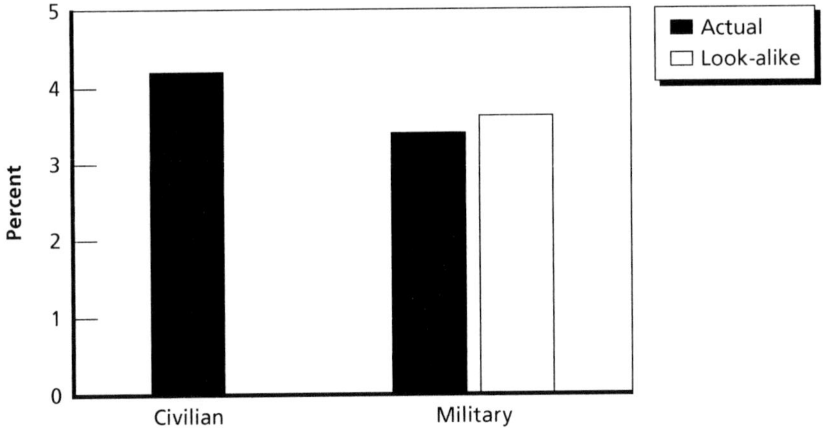

SOURCE: PUMS 2000.
RAND *MG566-4.8*

Relative Earnings of Military Husbands Living in Metropolitan Areas

We also compared the hourly wages of military and civilian husbands who live in the same MSAs. Similar to the previous chapter, the results presented in this section do account for possible differences in the observables. Comparing earnings in the same MSA ensures that any local labor market effects that may exist do not influence the national-level data. As we did with military wives, we first grouped all residents of each MSA into ten equal groups, based on their hourly wages. For instance, the first group represents the lowest wage earners and the tenth group refers to the highest wage earners within a MSA. Then we assigned each husband to a decile group based on his hourly wage. Thus, if the wages of military and civilian husbands have identical distributions across the decile groups, we would see overlapping lines in Figure 4.9.

Figure 4.9
Earnings of Military Husbands Compared with Those of Civilian Husbands Living in the Same MSA, 2000

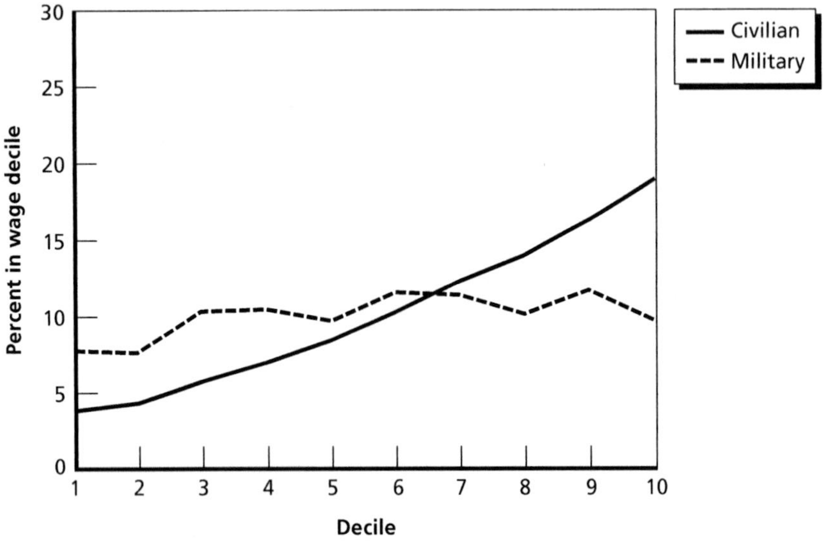

SOURCE: PUMS 2000.
RAND *MG566-4.9*

As can be seen in Figure 4.9, civilian husbands are underrepresented (less than 10 percent) among the low-wage deciles and overrepresented (more than 10 percent) among the high-wage deciles. The military husbands, on the other hand, are slightly underrepresented among the very low-wage deciles and equally distributed in the mid- to high-wage deciles. Cumulatively, more than 70 percent of civilian husbands belong to the top 50 percent of wage earners, whereas about 54 percent of military husbands belong in the same category.

Summary

In this chapter, we repeated most of the analyses we performed in Chapters Two and Three, but for husbands of military service members rather than wives. Because our sample size for husbands is smaller, we could not obtain reliable results at the level of the individual service, so we report differences between civilian husbands and military husbands as a whole.

Like military wives compared with civilian wives, military husbands tend to be more educated than civilian husbands, and they are more likely to have a young child at home and to move more often. They are also less likely to be white. Like military wives compared with civilian wives, military husbands have less favorable employment status and earnings than civilian husbands: They have slightly lower labor force participation and employment rates and a much higher unemployment rate.

The national wage-rate result is confirmed by the metropolitan-area analysis: Military husbands are more likely than civilian husbands to fall into the bottom 40 percent and less likely to fall into the top 30 percent. Relatively speaking, the distribution for military husbands was a little more favorable than that for military wives, a comparison also borne out in the national-level data.

Differences in background characteristics do not explain the small differences between military and civilian husbands in employment rate. They explain about half the difference in yearly income, most of the difference in unemployment rate, and almost all of the difference in hourly wage rate. In other words, although civilian husbands who look like military husbands are more likely to find jobs than civilian husbands, they tend to be paid less. This trend may be associated with observable factors such as education, race and mobility. Military husbands tend to be more educated than civilian husbands. They are, however, less likely to be white and more likely to relocate often. Both may have adverse impact on military husbands' wages.

Therefore, policy recommendations that are designed to address observable characteristics have the potential to partially eliminate the significant disparities in yearly income, unemployment rate, and hourly wage rate between military and civilian husbands. For employment disparities that cannot be attributed to observable characteristics, more data are needed to understand the causes and to develop programs and policies that will lessen the gaps.

CHAPTER FIVE

Conclusion

Our updated analysis using data from the 2000 census confirms findings previously reported in Harrell et al. (2004); the demographic and employment trends of military and civilian spouses from a decade before still hold true in general. Military spouses continue to be at a relative employment disadvantage in comparison to civilian spouses.

Harrell et al. (2004) recommend addressing military childcare availability and affordability, and Hosek et al. (2002) made recommendations regarding mobility and geographic location of military families. These two recommendations must be recognized as mechanisms designed to reduce the portion of employment disparities that can be explained by observable characteristics. Even if these policies and programs were enacted and were successful at reducing the gap in employment outcomes, they would not affect the portion of the gap that is caused by unobserved factors, such as employers' perception of military spouses and the spouses' "taste" for work. For instance, look-alike analyses of military wives' unemployment rates (see Figure S.2) suggest that policies and programs aimed at reducing unemployment rates of military wives may succeed in narrowing the observed gap. However, they will not eliminate the portion of the gap that is attributed to unobserved characteristics, to the extent that those are impractical to modify by policy changes or resistant to such changes.

An exception would be if observed characteristics are correlated with the unobserved factors. Then any improvements based on the observed characteristic may also improve the correlated unobserved factor, further reducing the employment disparities between military and civilian spouses. More data and analysis are needed to better understand what the unobserved factors are, how they may be correlated with other factors, and how they affect employment outcomes.

This study also found that certain employment outcomes may be more sensitive to policy interventions that are based on observable characteristics. One may see larger policy effects on military-civilian gaps that are partly or mostly explained by observable characteristics than on gaps that cannot be explained with available data. For instance, policies that target demographic disparities such as mobility, location, and childcare may significantly improve the unemployment rate of military wives, but the difference in military and civilian wives' hourly wages—attributed largely to unobserved characteristics—may remain unchanged. However, suppose that unobserved characteristics holding down military wives' hourly wages (and, to some extent, unemployment) were found to include a factor (e.g., employer discrimination based on the expectation of increased mobility) correlated with an observed characteristic (e.g., mobility). Then, addressing the observed characteristic in a manner perceivable by employers, such as advocacy campaigns or tax incentives for hiring military spouses, could mute the effect of the unobserved characteristic.

Clearly, there are unknowns that can be resolved through further inquiry: Some unobserved characteristics may be observed through instruments not yet developed or fielded, and our understanding of the relative importance of different observable factors can be refined and updated based on additional information. DoD, as well as the research community, continues to seek answers to the question of employment disparity between military and civilian spouses. Lim and Golinelli, 2006, for example, contribute to DoD's data collection efforts by determining valid measures of labor market conditions for military spouses and the sample size that is sufficient for generalizability. Our aggregate analysis and that of its predecessor thus take only the first steps. Further work will be required to sort out the influences on military spouses' employment conditions.

APPENDIX

Results of Statistical Analysis

Table A.1.a
Balance Table for Military and Civilian Wives Comparison, Army

Variable	Army	Civilian Propensity Score—Weighted	Civilian
Wife Characteristics			
Age	32.18	32.36	40.14
Race (%)			
African-American	17.5	17.5	6.8
Hispanic	12.3	12.3	12.6
Asian	5.9	5.9	5.7
Native American	1.4	1.4	0.9
White	62.4	62.5	73.5
Other	0.5	0.4	0.5
Education (%)			
No high school diploma/GED	5.3	5.3	14.5
High school diploma/GED	25.8	25.1	27
Some college	45.7	45.8	30
Bachelor's degree	17.6	17.5	19.2
Graduate school	5.6	6.3	9.2
School enrollment (%)			
Not attending school	87.8	87.7	93.8
Enrolled in public school	10.1	10.2	4.7
Enrolled in private school	2.1	2.1	1.4
Move in past five years (%)			
No move	11.8	12.8	53.9
Intrastate	16.3	15.8	35
Interstate	58.6	58.5	7.9
From abroad	13.3	12.9	3.2
Young child at home (%)	46	47	29
Nonmetropolitan residence (%)	17	17	17

Table A.1.a—Continued

Variable	Army	Civilian Propensity Score—Weighted	Civilian
Husband Characteristics			
Age	33.28	33.59	42.31
Race (%)			
African-American	20.5	20.3	7.1
Hispanic	10.1	9.9	12.4
Asian	3.3	3.4	5.4
Native American	1.3	1.2	0.9
White	64.6	64.9	73.7
Other	0.3	0.3	0.5
Education (%)			
No high school diploma/GED	1	2.1	17.7
High school diploma/GED	19.4	19.3	25.5
Some college	51	50.2	25.5
Bachelor's degree	16.8	16.9	18.9
Graduate school	11.8	11.6	12.5
School enrollment (%)			
Not attending school	86.7	86.7	95.5
Enrolled in public school	10.2	10.2	3.3
Enrolled in private school	3.1	3.1	1.2
Income	$33,989.25	$35,310.09	$43,221.07

Table A.1.b
Balance Table for Military and Civilian Wives Comparison, Air Force

Variable	Air Force	Civilian Propensity Score—Weighted	Civilian
Wife Characteristics			
Age	33.53	33.61	40.14
Race (%)			
African-American	8.2	8.3	6.8
Hispanic	8.5	8.7	12.6
Asian	7	8.	5.7
Native American	1.2	1.2	0.9
White	74.9	74.7	73.5
Other	0.2	0.2	0.5
Education (%)			
No high school diploma/GED	4.2	4	14.5
High school diploma/GED	21.7	21.7	27
Some college	45.4	45.2	30
Bachelor's degree	22.5	22.5	19.2
Graduate school	6.2	6.7	9.2

Table A.1.b—Continued

Variable	Air Force	Civilian Propensity Score—Weighted	Civilian
School enrollment (%)			
Not attending school	87.1	86.8	93.8
Enrolled in public school	11	11.1	4.7
Enrolled in private school	2	2.1	1.4
Move in past five years (%)			
No move	14.1	14.9	53.9
Intrastate	18.3	17.9	35
Interstate	55.3	54.9	7.9
From abroad	12.4	12.3	3.2
Young child at home (%)	43	43	29
Nonmetropolitan residence (%)	11	12	17
Husband Characteristics			
Age	34.45	34.7	42.31
Race (%)			
African-American	10.1	10	7.1
Hispanic	6.1	6.5	12.4
Asian	2.7	2.8	5.4
Native American	1	0.9	0.9
White	79.8	79.4	73.7
Other	0.3	0.3	0.5
Education (%)			
No high school diploma/GED	0.4	1.4	17.7
High school diploma/GED	11.9	11.7	25.5
Some college	52	51.5	25.5
Bachelor's degree	15.3	15.3	18.9
Graduate school	20.4	20.2	12.5
School enrollment (%)			
Not attending school	84.2	84.3	95.5
Enrolled in public school	11.8	11.7	3.3
Enrolled in private school	4.0	4.1	1.2
Income	$37,428.05	$38,606.8	$43,221.07

Table A.1.c
Balance Table for Military and Civilian Wives Comparison, Navy

Variable	Navy	Civilian Propensity Score—Weighted	Civilian
Wife Characteristics			
Age	33.09	33.12	40.14
Race (%)			
African-American	12.1	12	6.8
Hispanic	8.6	8.8	12.6
Asian	11.5	11	5.7
Native American	1.2	1.2	0.9
White	66	65.8	73.5
Other	0.7	0.6	0.5
Education (%)			
No high school diploma/GED	6	5.9	14.5
High school diploma/GED	25.1	25.3	27
Some college	43.7	43.6	30
Bachelor's degree	19.2	18.9	19.2
Graduate school	5.9	6.3	9.2
School enrollment (%)			
Not attending school	87.8	87.8	93.8
Enrolled in public school	9.8	9.9	4.7
Enrolled in private school	2.4	2.3	1.4
Move in past five years (%)			
No move	16.1	16.6	53.9
Intrastate	23.7	23.4	35
Interstate	52.8	52.5	7.9
From abroad	7.4	7.5	3.2
Young child at home (%)	44	44	29
Nonmetropolitan residence (%)	6	7	17
Husband Characteristics			
Age	33.74	33.97	42.31
Race (%)			
African-American	13.7	13.7	7.1
Hispanic	8.1	8.4	12.4
Asian	6	6	5.4
Native American	1.1	1.1	0.9
White	70.7	70.5	73.7
Other	0.4	0.4	0.5
Education (%)			
No high school diploma/GED	1.4	2.3	17.7
High school diploma/GED	26.6	26.5	25.5
Some college	45.8	45.7	25.5
Bachelor's degree	15.5	15.2	18.9
Graduate school	10.7	10.2	12.5

Table A.1.c—Continued

Variable	Navy	Civilian Propensity Score—Weighted	Civilian
School enrollment (%)			
Not attending school	87.1	86.9	95.5
Enrolled in public school	9.3	9.5	3.3
Enrolled in private school	3.6	3.6	1.2
Income	$36,156.63	$37,203.14	$43,221.07

Table A.1.d
Balance Table for Military and Civilian Wives Comparison, Marine Corps

Variable	Marine	Civilian Propensity Score—Weighted	Civilian
Wife Characteristics			
Age	29.83	30.2	40.14
Race (%)			
African-American	11.7	11.4	6.8
Hispanic	12.5	12	12.6
Asian	6.7	6.5	5.7
Native American	1.6	1.6	0.9
White	67.3	68.1	73.5
Other	0.2	0.3	0.5
Education (%)			
No high school diploma/GED	5.8	6.7	14.5
High school diploma/GED	26.9	26.3	27
Some college	47.3	46	30
Bachelor's degree	15.9	16.1	19.2
Graduate school	4.1	4.9	9.2
School enrollment (%)			
Not attending school	86.9	86.9	93.8
Enrolled in public school	10.5	10.5	4.7
Enrolled in private school	2.6	2.6	1.4
Move in past five years (%)			
No move	8.7	10.8	53.9
Intrastate	22.3	21.4	35
Interstate	62.6	61.5	7.9
From abroad	6.4	6.3	3.2
Young child at home (%)	46	47	29
Nonmetropolitan residence (%)	14	15	17

Table A.1.d—Continued

Variable	Marine	Civilian Propensity Score—Weighted	Civilian
Husband Characteristics			
Age	30.55	31.14	42.31
Race (%)			
African-American	14.1	13.6	7.1
Hispanic	13.1	12.5	12.4
Asian	1.9	2.8	5.4
Native American	1.9	1.9	0.9
White	68.6	68.8	73.7
Other	0.4	0.4	0.5
Education (%)			
No high school diploma/GED	1.5	3.7	17.7
High school diploma/GED	36.3	34.6	25.5
Some college	41.2	41.1	25.5
Bachelor's degree	15.1	15.3	18.9
Graduate school	6	5.4	12.5
School enrollment (%)			
Not attending school	87.4	87.2	95.5
Enrolled in public school	8.9	8.9	3.3
Enrolled in private school	3.8	3.9	1.2
Income	$31,683.73	$33,931.11	$43,221.07

Table A.2.a
Summary Statistics of Labor Market Outcomes for Military and Civilian Wives, Army

Variable	Army	Civilian Propensity Score—Weighted	Civilian
Yearly income	$11,566.1	$16,821.2 p<.001	$18,591.07 p<.001
Hourly wage	$8.72	$11.22 p<.001	$11.90 p<.001
Weeks worked	26.84	33.47 p<.001	33.03 p<.001
Employed	54.01%	66.15% p<.001	65.43% p<.001
Unemployed	5.46%	4.0% p=.015	2.3% p<.001
Not in the labor force	40.52%	29.84% p<.001	32.21% p<.001

Table A.2.b
Summary Statistics of Labor Market Outcomes for Military and Civilian Wives, Air Force

Variable	Air Force	Civilian Propensity Score—Weighted	Civilian
Yearly income	$12,323.2	$17,546.7 p<.001	$18,591.07 p<.001
Hourly wage	$8.52	$11.62 p<.001	$11.9 p<.001
Weeks worked	28.37	33.43 p<.001	33.03 p<.001
Employed	58.14%	66.67% p<.001	65.43% p<.001
Unemployed	3.5%	3.2% not significant	2.3% p<.001
Not in the labor force	38.36%	30.12% p<.001	32.21% p<.001

Table A.2.c
Summary Statistics of Labor Market Outcomes for Military and Civilian Wives, Navy

Variable	Navy	Civilian Propensity Score—Weighted	Civilian
Yearly income	$12,836.3	$18,065.6 p<.001	$18,591.07 p<.001
Hourly wage	$9.26	$11.97 p<.001	$11.9 p<.001
Weeks worked	28.81	34.57 p<.001	33.03 p<.001
Employed	58.0%	68.13% p<.001	65.43% p<.001
Unemployed	4.64%	3.31%	2.3% p<.001
Not in the labor force	37.36%	28.55% p<.001	32.21% p<.001

Table A.2.d
Summary Statistics of Labor Market Outcomes for Military and Civilian Wives, Marine Corps

Variable	Marine Corps	Civilian Propensity Score—Weighted	Civilian
Yearly income	$11,281.2	$16,086.2 p<.001	$18,591.07 p<.001
Hourly wage	$8.69	$10.88 p<.001	$11.90 p<.001
Weeks worked	27.38	24.13 p<.001	33.03 p<.001
Employed	55.71%	67.43% p<.001	65.43% p<.001
Unemployed	4.9%	3.9% p=0.07	2.3% p<.001
Not in the labor force	39.3%	28.68% p<.001	32.21% p<.001

Table A.3
Balance Table for Military and Civilian Husbands Comparison

Variable	Military	Civilian Propensity Score—Weighted	Civilian
Husband Characteristics			
Age	35.5	35.66	44.08
Race (%)			
African-American	28.2	27.7	7.2
Hispanic	8.1	8.3	10.4
Asian	2.6	2.9	4.3
Native American	1.5	1.5	0.9
White	59.3	59.2	76.9
Other	0.2	0.3	0.4
Education (%)			
No high school diploma/GED	4.1	5.4	14.8
High school diploma/GED	24.2	23.8	26.8
Some college	49.2	48.4	28.4
Bachelor's degree	13.3	13.3	18.2
Graduate school	9.2	9.2	11.9
School enrollment (%)			
Not attending school	85.8	85.8	95.7
Enrolled in public school	11.2	11.4	3.2
Enrolled in private school	3	2.8	1.1

Table A.3—Continued

Variable	Military	Civilian Propensity Score—Weighted	Civilian
Move in past five years (%)			
No move	17.2	18.3	56.6
Interstate	21.9	21.4	33.1
Across states	51	50.4	8.2
From abroad	9.8	9.9	2.1
Young child at home (%)	41	41	25
Nonmetropolitan residence (%)	11	12	17
Wife Characteristics			
Age	33.22	33.53	41.93
Race (%)			
African-American	25.7	25.5	6.7
Hispanic	7.9	8.1	10.6
Asian	3.7	3.9	4.9
Native American	1.9	1.8	1
White	60.5	60.5	76.4
Other	0.3	0.3	0.4
Education (%)			
No high school diploma/GED	1.7	3.1	13.2
High school diploma/GED	15.5	15.6	28.8
Some college	53.2	52.9	31.1
Bachelor's degree	16.1	15.1	18.2
Graduate school	13.4	13.2	8.8
School enrollment (%)			
Not attending school	79.6	79.6	94.3
Enrolled in public school	16.0	15.9	4.4
Enrolled in private school	4.4	4.5	1.3
Income	$27,884.22	$28,040.97	$18,570.2

Table A.4
Summary Statistics of Labor Market Outcomes for Military and Civilian Husbands

Variable	Military	Civilian Propensity Score—Weighted	Civilian
Yearly income	$29,536.9	$37,089.8 p<.001	$42,868.7 p<.001
Hourly wage	$16.91	$17.98 not significant	$20.92 p<.001
Weeks worked	41.49	45.7 p<.001	44.35 p<.001
Employed	79.91%	87.27% p<.001	83.95 p<.001
Unemployed	4.3%	3% p=0.014	2.2% p<.001
Not in the labor force	15.77%	9.71% p<.001	13.83% p=.035

Bibliography

Barsky, Robert, John Bound, Kerwin Kofi Charles, and Joseph P. Lupton, "Accounting for the Black-White Wealth Gap: A Nonparametric Approach," *Journal of the American Statistical Association,* Vol. 97, 2002, pp. 663–673.

Browne, Irene, ed., *Latinas and African American Women at Work: Race, Gender, and Economic Inequality,* New York: Russell Sage Foundation, 1999.

Coser, Lewis A., *Greedy Institutions: Patterns of Undivided Commitment,* New York: The Free Press, 1974.

Day, Jennifer Cheeseman, National Population Projections, U.S. Census Bureau, 2001. As of December 5, 2006:
http://www.census.gov/population/www/pop-profile/natproj.html

Grossman, Allyson Sherman, "The Employment Situation for Military Wives," *Monthly Labor Review,* Vol. 104, 1981, pp. 60–64.

Harrell, Margaret C., Nelson Lim, Laura Werber Castaneda, and Daniela Golinelli, *Working Around the Military: Challenges to Military Spouse Employment and Education,* Santa Monica, Calif.: RAND Corporation, MG-196-OSD, 2004.

Hayghe, Howard, "Military and Civilian Wives: Update on the Labor Force Gap," *Monthly Labor Review,* Vol. 82, No. 2, Pt. 2, 1974, pp. S136–S163.

Henderson, Kristin, *While They're At War: The True Story of American Families on the Homefront,* Boston: Houghton Mifflin Co., 2006.

Higganbotham, Elizabeth, and Mary Romero, eds., *Women and Work: Exploring Race, Ethnicity, and Class,* Vol. 6 of Women and Work: A Research and Policy Series, Thousand Oaks, Calif.: Sage, 1997.

Hodge, Robert W., "Toward a Theory of Racial Differences in Employment," *Social Forces,* Vol. 52, No. 1, September, 1973, pp. 16–31.

Hosek, James, Beth Asch, C. Christine Fair, Craig Martin, and Michael Mattock, *Married to the Military; The Employment and Earnings of Military Wives Compared with Those of Civilian Wives,* Santa Monica, Calif.: RAND Corporation, MR-1565-OSD, 2002.

Lichter, Daniel T., and Zhenchao Qian, *Marriage and Family in a Multiracial Society,* Washington, D.C.: Population Reference Bureau, 2004.

Lim, Nelson, and Daniela Golinelli, *Monitoring Employment Conditions of Military Spouses,* Santa Monica, Calif.: RAND Corporation, TR-324, 2006.

Mare, Robert D., "Five Decades of Educational Assortative Mating," *American Sociological Review,* No. 56, 1991, pp. 15–32.

Martel, Jennifer L., and Laura A. Kelter, "The Job Market Remains Strong in 1999," Monthly Labor Review, February 2000, pp. 3–23.

McCaffrey, Daniel F., Greg Ridgeway, and Andrew R. Morral, "Propensity Score Estimation With Boosted Regression for Evaluating Causal Effects in Observational Studies," *Psychological Methods,* Vol. 9, No. 4, 2004, pp. 403–425.

Neal, Derek. 2004. "Is the Measured Black-White Wage Gap Among Women Too Small?" *Journal of Political Economy,* Vol. 112, No. 1, pp. S1–S28.

Payne, Deborah M., John T. Warner, and Roger D. Little, "Tied Migration and Returns to Human Capital: The Case of Military Wives," *Social Science Quarterly,* Vol. 73, No. 2, June 1992, pp. 329–339.

Pryor, F. L., and D. Schaffer, "Wages and the University Educated: A Paradox Resolved," *Monthly Labor Review,* July 1997, pp. 3–18.

Reskin, Barbara F., and Patricia A. Roos, *Job Queues, Gender Queues: Explaining Women's Inroads into Male Occupations,* Philadelphia: Temple University Press, 1990.

Schwartz, Brad J., Lisa L. Wood, and Janet D. Griffith, "The Impact of Military Life on Spouse Labor Force Outcomes," *Armed Forces and Society,* Vol. 17, No. 3, 1991, pp. 385–407.

Segal, Mady Wechsler, "The Military and the Family as Greedy Institutions," *Armed Forces & Society,* Vol. 13, No. 1, 1986, pp. 9–38.

Thurow, Lester C., *Generating Inequality: Mechanisms of Distribution in the U.S. Economy,* New York: Basic Books, Inc., 1975.

U.S. Department of Defense, *Overview of the 1999 Survey of Spouses of Active Duty Personnel,* Washington, D.C.: Defense Manpower Data Center, Report No. 2000-014, February 2002.

———, *Modernized Social Compact,* Washington, D.C.: U.S. Department of Defense, May 2004a.

———, *Report of the 1st Quadrennial Quality of Life Review,* Washington, D.C.: U.S. Department of Defense, May 2004b.

Wardynski, E. Casey, *Military Compensation in the Age of Two-Income Households: Adding Spouses' Earnings to the Compensation Policy Mix,* Santa Monica, Calif.: RAND Corporation, RGSD-154, 2000.

Wolff, E., "Technology and the Demand for Skills," in L. Borghans and A. de Grip, eds., *The Overeducated Worker? The Economics of Skill Utilization*, Northampton, Mass.: Edward Elgar Publishers, 2000.